About the author

Jack Léon Mackey is twenty-eight years old, and from Tunbridge Wells, Kent.

DELIRIUM

Jack Léon Mackey

DELIRIUM

Vanguard Press

VANGUARD PAPERBACK

© Copyright 2023
Jack Léon Mackey

The right of Jack Léon Mackey to be identified as author of this work has been asserted by him in accordance with the Copyright, Designs and Patents Act 1988.

All Rights Reserved

No reproduction, copy or transmission of this publication may be made without written permission.
No paragraph of this publication may be reproduced, copied or transmitted save with the written permission of the publisher, or in accordance with the provisions of the Copyright Act 1956 (as amended).

Any person who commits any unauthorised act in relation to this publication may be liable to criminal prosecution and civil claims for damages.

A CIP catalogue record for this title is available from the British Library.

ISBN 978-1-80016-468-0

Vanguard Press is an imprint of
Pegasus Elliot Mackenzie Publishers Ltd.
www.pegasuspublishers.com

First Published in 2023

Vanguard Press
Sheraton House Castle Park
Cambridge England

Printed & Bound in Great Britain

Dedication

To my family, friends and most importantly, my mum. I wouldn't be here without you.

Acknowledgements

With thanks to the NHS staff of Pembury hospital and the amazing people at Bridge House detox centre. I am forever grateful. Also thank you to the people who helped to make this book happen. This wouldn't be possible without you.

Cover and illustrations by Abbie Sibun.

Prologue

I'm lying awake in bed. It's pitch black, and my brain is in overdrive. It happens from time to time. Some of the things I've experienced weigh on my mind and I have trouble trying to figure out what it all means if it means anything at all. So I thought I would write it down. A friend of mine, who unfortunately isn't here anymore, told me that when he put pen to paper about his emotions and experiences it helped him make sense of the inexplicable things in his life. This is what I'm going to try to do.

Chapter 1: Education

I had been drinking very excessively. It started, as most mistakes do, with ignorance. I never understood how someone could become so dependent on a liquid; it just didn't make any sense to me at all. I had, as with most of the population, given in to the misconceptions of alcoholism and its affects. I just thought, "Just stop, if it hurts, don't do it." But as I came to learn all too well, that isn't up to you if you reach a certain point.

I had begun not being able to sleep. That's how it's started for me. I would lie awake all night, anxiety coursing through my body, my brain rapidly shifting in all directions, depicting my worst fears possible, my worst memories, and playing them on repeat in my head. The shaking was there, but the shaking had been there a while. Eating was becoming challenging.

I remember having a phone conversation with my sister, explaining how I couldn't even keep down toast. Every time I ate, it was like my body and my brain rejected it. I would start violently shaking; I could feel my heart in my chest, pounding as if it was going to burst. My body worked so hard to digest food that it literally took everything out of me. After eating (if I could) a slice of toast I would rest for as much time as possible.

By this time I was drinking up to twelve litres of cider a day. If I didn't ingest alcohol within half an hour of the last drink I would start withdrawing. Unfortunately, after going to my local addiction help service and then swiftly to hospital, I was told grimly about my bodily dependence to alcohol. I had had a sleepless night, shaking so much from anxiety and withdrawal that I was panicking. I suffered seizures and had to be rushed to hospital by my gran.

At hospital they gave me some Librium and informed me of what was happening and sent me home. Being told that my body was dependent was at first a green light to drink to me. I was twenty-two years old and I didn't want to stop. I didn't want reality; reality was boring and everything was better drunk.

After coming home from the hospital things became much worse over the weeks. I ate very rarely; my stomach expanded due to the alcohol I was consuming but everywhere else on my body, weight just fell off. I wasn't sleeping, and if I did I would have to use Zopiclone and a lot of drink to get an hour or so.

The day that changed a lot of things started pretty normally. I woke up at five-thirty in the morning, shaking so badly I could barely walk, downed a couple of pints of cider and retreated to the spare room in the house to sit and drink. It killed my family and friends seeing me this way and they have been the most supportive, loving people I have been lucky enough to have in my life, but by this stage it was dangerous for me *not* to drink due to withdrawal.

The day went on as normal. I drank around eight litres of cider and by the time evening came I was still only half cut.

I lay in bed. Tingling, itching, and scratching. I assumed I had got bed bugs, as this is quite obviously that. I get up, strip my bed, go upstairs and tell my mum about it and change my sheets. The itching and tingling continue.

I try and ignore it as it must be just from our dog or something to do with that. I lay in bed trying to sleep with my fan on next to my bed, when suddenly I can hear singing. Not normal singing but the type of singing that I can only describe as Russian military singing.

Writing this and seeing it written down it seems mental, but unfortunately that was just the beginning of it.

I tried my best to figure out where the singing was coming from. I thought it must be coming from outside or a phone somewhere or someone else in the house.

It's coming from my fan. I put my ear up to the fan blades as they spin round and the sound coming from it is military marching music.

I start to panic. I'm alone in my dark room and I start to panic more than I ever have in my entire life.

This isn't normal? *This isn't normal!* Why can I hear that? This is not right. I run upstairs, knock on my mum's bedroom door and ask her to come to my room to show her.

She hears nothing and is quite obviously very confused and concerned. She tries to calm me down and sits on my bed while I am hyperventilating with my head in a pillow.

She tells me she will stay in my room, as I beg her not to leave. I'm terrified, and I don't know what is happening. I keep repeating to her, "I've lost it, that's it, isn't it? I've finally lost it?"

She tells me it's perfectly normal if I haven't been sleeping enough, people hear things. This gives me some comfort but the anxiety and panic is still there, and so is the singing.

I turn off my fan and lie in my bed as my mum sits next to me, calming me as I try to sleep.

I open and shut my eyes as I am laying on my back on my bed, and I can see streams of light, flowing through my room, starting through my blinds, and floating around my room, extremely slowly.

I panic again and shut my eyes tight, telling my mum everything I'm seeing and hearing. The singing has returned, but this time it's an ominous chant, the type of chant you would hear in *The Wicker Man* before a sacrifice scene, something out of a horror film. It's coming from outside, but I cannot pinpoint where from; it sounds far away but getting closer.

I tell my mum all this and by this stage, I am bolt upright on my bed panicking. She leaves the room and tells me she will call the NHS helpline to see what to do.

But things by this point are rapidly accelerating. I can see, out of my landing window, over fifty hooded figures with lit torches coming round the road next to my house, approaching my drive. I am running from the landing to my mum, to the window, to my mum, to the kitchen.

I grab a knife from the kitchen side and I hold it with me near my front door. I look down at my hands and notice what looks like a silky substance is threading out of my fingertips. I have to look closely but I can see it, very fine, almost like looking at a silver thread, slowly coming out of my fingertips.

I start to think that something is now happening to my body. Is this linked? Am I hearing things and seeing lights in my room, feeling and seeing silver thread out of my fingers all linked to these hooded figures outside? Are they coming to the house to take me? Why can no one else see what I'm seeing? It's clear as day! As clear as my mum standing in front of me telling me there is nothing there. I can hear them knocking on the windows; I see shadows of hands on the front door glass. They are trying to get to me. All I can hear is their chanting and knocking on the window.

My mum tells me we are going for a drive, "To get away from what is happening." I am scared, more scared than ever, but I agree and leave the front door with the knife.

They aren't at the front door anymore; they are round the corner and I can see them coming down our road. I scream to my mum to get in the car and we begin to drive off.

I look at my hands and not only am I seeing the silver thread coming out of my fingers but I am seeing red marks, almost like messages, forming on my palms. I rub them away and they come back, forming with the blood under my skin.

I look in the mirror and something is changing with my face; my eyes are changing colour, my teeth are being replaced by new straighter teeth and I can hear voices coming from somewhere I can't see telling me that this is all to prepare me.

"I don't see them following us," I tell my mum and she tells me to please try and calm down.

We arrive at the hospital. I assume this is to help me get away from the figures who came to my house and to get me help with my body, which by this stage is changing completely before my eyes. We wait for a long time; I go to the toilet and feel that something has happened to my urine. The same silvery thread that was coming out of my fingers is now coming out of my genitals.

I go out to the waiting area and tell my mum this new information. She tells me everything is going to be all right and to sit tight and wait. After we are seen, me and my mum are taken to a separate waiting area beyond the front desk and asked to stay in there.

I'm assuming, looking back, this is because my behaviour had become extremely worrying.

My mum sits in with me worried sick. I'm pacing the room, talking to the voice that has been speaking to me since the car, telling me I can take one person with me away from Earth. I am in a state of panic, confusion and desperation. Trying to desperately explain to my mum the situation and that they will be coming to take us soon and she needs to be ready.

A doctor comes into the room and tries to speak to me but I am busy in the corner speaking to the voice. He sits and speaks to my mum.

My mum begs me to sit down, and says she needs to speak to me.

She tells me everything I've been experiencing is in my head, which she went along with it to keep me calm but, it is in my head.

I cannot even describe how it felt to hear that. My whole world crumbled around me and it left me feeling so scared and alone. All these things I've seen and heard weren't real. The things I'm continuing to hear are all in my head.

The doctor explains to me this is because of something called 'delirium tremens' and I am having severe alcohol withdrawal.

I am taken through to a temporary ward where I am told to lay on a bed. My heartbeat is so fast I feel I could die. My mum doesn't leave my side.

I stare at the ceiling and small cracks in the paintwork are warping, contorting into fast paced cartoons dancing above me. Strange images of distorted small figures acting out nasty scenarios. Every piece of my being is screaming out, my body is shutting down. I'm having auditory hallucinations along with visual, and even closing my eyes does nothing to stop the nightmare.

I grip my mum's hand as I lay on the hospital bed. I tell her I love her and I'm sorry, and that I'm scared, I don't want to die, but if I do, I'm sorry.

She stays strong, tears rolling down her cheeks, but her face filled with hope.

A doctor comes in after I am fitted with a cannula. My vitals are checked and my heartbeat is high but they are going to keep me in for a detox.

This is music to my ears. Up until this point my life had been a living hell, waking up after an hour's sleep a night, so weak and sick, shaking uncontrollably and not being able to walk properly until I inhale enough cider to keep my withdrawal at bay. Countless trips to the hospital, coming home, crying, throwing up bile every hour of the day, back crippled with pain from my kidneys, liver shutting down.

A hospital detox is not something they hand out, so I was very lucky to get the help. I cry with joy and sadness at the mess of where I am but the prospect of getting my life back again.

I am taken through to another bed, until I am taken to my ward.

My mum has gone to speak to the doctors, and I am alone.

I am seeing figures, outlines of silver, forming a body, walking in all directions around the corridors and coming towards my bed.

A cold, thin looking outline peers over me as I lie on my bed. I stare through it, towards the ceiling. This isn't real; I've been told this isn't real.

It seems to notice I am not giving it attention and moves away. This happens on and off for an hour. I occasionally talk to them, ask them why they are here, and they look at me so distantly, as if I'm not close but so far away. They sometimes reply, but what I hear is quieter than a whisper; they get frustrated and I can see the figures shouting, but it's still just a whisper.

I am put into a wheelchair as I am now struggling to walk due to my shaking. The doctor accompanies us to the ward I will be staying in. As soon as I look in the room I see four dark, small, demonic looking creatures waiting for me. They are about a foot tall and are staring at me menacingly through the door. I explain to my mum and the doctor what I am seeing, what I am hearing; the doctor tells me firmly it isn't real, there is nothing there. He strikes me as very irritated; another alcoholic hallucinating, I have better things to be doing, is what I'm feel coming from his body language. He probably does have better things to be doing, and I feel ashamed, and so vulnerable I feel I could crack.

I am taken into the room where my mum shows me around, but I am trying hard to get rid of the things I can see. I look towards the door and I see a figure at the glass, dark, tall and menacing. He puts his thumb to his neck and draws it across his throat, staring at me with pure aggression and malice. I shout and scream and in that moment I feel scared for my life. This may not be real to anyone else, but to me, I can see and hear and feel these things and I am beside myself with desperation. I pull my cannula from my hand and shout that I need to leave, I cannot be here as these things will kill me. I haven't slept in days, so sick and deprived of anything but acidic cider, burning my throat and guts every day, I just can't bear it any longer.

A doctor and two nurses fly into the room, talking to my mum and the doctor telling me to sit on the bed. I cannot think of anything but getting out of the room and into safety from these creatures that are haunting me. A needle enters my arm, the doctor is telling me to relax and to calm down. Everything goes black.

Chapter 2: Hospital

I wake up.

I don't know what happened, everything feels brighter and out of focus.

My mum sits asleep in a chair to the left of me, as a nurse comes into my room, she stirs. It's six-thirty a.m.

The nurse connects my cannula to a Pabrinex bag that hangs just behind my head, and checks to see how I am feeling.

I say that that is the first time I have slept in weeks. She smiles and laughs.

She explains that what I was given was a strong sedative, as my hallucinations were causing me to lose control and upset other patients. I apologize for this and feel very ashamed. She tells me not to feel embarrassed, she gives me my dose of Librium and walks away.

In front of me sits, on a tray, two slices of toast, a cup of coffee, some butter and a carton of orange juice.

I still can't eat, I don't feel like I can yet.

I still feel like I'm in a lucid dream.

Almost immediately the hallucinations start.

The dark creatures from the day before have dissipated, leaving different forms in their place.

What I now see is a small, excitable, childlike man. He must be, again, only around a foot tall, or less.

He flits from one place in the room to the other, laughing and giggling excitably. As I watch him dance around my room, I notice as he does, he is creating beautiful murals of intricate artwork on my room wall. Pasted onto the wall in a scribbling motion, the images of large flowers, gigantic mouths of reddened alcoholic men guzzling comical amounts of beer with three Xs on the bottle, characters much like himself are dancing around in a circle holding hands, birds flying, music notes and the list goes on. It appears on the wall as art and as he stops, the art turns to cartoon, and life springs into each illustration like lightning. I lay on my bed watching the wall in marvel.

I ask who he is, this small, strange character.

He looks at me, then in the blink of an eye appears sitting on the end of my bed. He calls himself 'Super Alex'; again, when spoken it sounds like a whisper, like someone has recorded themselves shouting then turned the volume right down. I struggle to hear and ask again, and he responds, "I am Super Alex," and he smiles, then disappears. I start scouting the room erratically for signs of him, but he is nowhere to be seen. The illustrations on the wall stay exactly where they are.

I don't understand this. If this isn't real, how can I take my eyes away from the wall, even close my eyes, and when I look again the exact images are still there, exactly how they were.

It's very confusing and makes me anxious.

My mum is awake by this point and looks slightly worried. I tell her what I have just seen, and that he called himself Super Alex. I ask her, if this is a hallucination, why have I never in my life seen anything remotely like what I'm seeing?

She shrugs and tells me the mind is an incredible thing. She is right, of course, who knows what goes through our minds.

I am starting to learn that the brain is a very sensitive thing.

My brother and sister come to visit me in hospital. They have always been incredibly supportive and they are over the moon I'm finally getting help. I explain that I'm feeling slightly better but still hallucinating. They bring me gifts and magazines to keep me busy and sit with me while they talk to my mum about what's happened.

I just feel exhausted. Every piece of me is aching. My lower back is in excruciating pain, I have a scan today to see if there is damage to my liver. The doctor came and visited me again to inform me of this.

He has a very no-nonsense way of explaining things to me, tough love, my mum calls it. I am scared and anxious and I can't take his harsh comments about my recklessness.

He prods my stomach and tells me it was a very close call, and that I need to stop now as I was very lucky to survive this.

I begin to cry when he leaves the room. Helpless, ashamed and weak, I lie in bed in tears with my mum by my side.

Night comes around fast.

As fast as the hallucinations go, they come. I am engulfed at night-time by dark imps, small creatures that crawl around my room, hissing, biting me, whispering terrifying threats that only I can hear.

I feel the pain on my skin when they bite. I do not know how this is possible, maybe because my brain believes it to be real; it is sending signals to my pain receptors that this is happening.

I am frantic once more. I pace the room, trying to stamp on these strange spectres, but every time I come close to thinking I've made one disappear, they appear again. The figure is outside my door again. Eyes glowing, thumb drawing itself across its throat, every time out gaze meets.

The night-time is the hardest. It brings with it not only the darkness in light, but the darkness in my mind. Things that only live in my nightmares are now visible, prowling the corridors in packs, or lone spectres, looking lost and scared, looking to me for answers that I can't give.

The nurse is called into my room where she witnesses me trying to stamp on the things I'm seeing. She explains they need to up my Librium dose, which will help with the hallucinations. She gives me some medication for my anxiety and after ten minutes I feel myself calming down.

My mum stays with me, holding my hand and telling me things will be okay.

I lay awake, in a trance of anxiety and numbness. I feel the weight of something at the end of my hospital bed and look down to find he is there. Super Alex sits staring and smiling at me; he winks and tells me he is sorry he left. I ask him where he went, and he replies, "You can't know that, you wouldn't understand." I find this confusing but don't ask again, as I am not sure I want to know the answer. He continues doing the illustrations I witnessed earlier again on the wall.

He stops, and I see him sway over to the corner of the room and begin to cry.

I ask him why he is crying; he doesn't respond.

I begin to get anxious and upset and ask him over and over why he is upset.

He shouts back, but I can barely hear what he responds. "I killed her, it wasn't my fault."

I ask him to come towards me, I can't hear what he is saying. He sits on my bed in tears; the tears spout from his eyes and fly off his face as if they were drawn from a cartoon.

I ask him what he means. I ask a few times. He seems inconsolable, as if something dark has come over him and he cannot break free of it.

He turns to me and says, "I can show you."

When he says this, I don't remember or know how, but I'm looking at a completely different surrounding. As if him saying that triggered it, I am standing in a small room, dark with faint lamps lit in the corner. Two figures are in a bed, having sex. I can't see who they are but they are the same sort of height as Super Alex. Now I think of it everything in this room is to the scale of his frame. There is a bathroom door to the left of me, and I am standing in the bedroom. I hear banging on what appears to be the front door, which is to the left of the bed. The two figures in bed begin to panic. I still can't see their faces.

A small person crashes through the front door, and advances on the two in bed.

He begins to viciously swipe and stab at the covers, with an extremely large knife. This continues for around five minutes, stabbing, screaming, stabbing, and crying. It then stops.

I can hear sobbing, as faint as if it's coming from a child. The person standing over the bed is crying, head in his hands, blood all over his face and torso.

He turns to me and advances on the bathroom door.

I recognise his face. It is Super Alex. His face is dark and blood stained. He rushes into the bathroom and locks the door. I hear crying, very faint again, coming from the inside of the bathroom. He is pleading, asking for help from someone. He tells himself he didn't mean it, he loved her. He tells himself he doesn't want to be here anymore and screams in such a way I feel his emotional pain.

I hear a gunshot.

As if hit by lightning I am snapped out of it. I am standing by my bathroom door in my hospital room, my mum standing by my bed asking me what I'm doing, who I'm talking to. I break down in tears and tell her what I've just seen, what just happened.

I am emotionally exhausted. I don't know what's real anymore. I am trapped in the nightmare world that I just cannot wake from; around every corner is something disturbing.

I lie down in bed and close my eyes. The nurse comes in and fixes a new bag of Pabrinex to my cannula, gives me a high dose of Librium with a sedative. I fall asleep.

Chapter 3: Phantoms and figures

I wake around five a.m., mouth dry and bed soaked in sweat. I'm trembling and feel panic. I call for a nurse and she comes in and tells me I snored a lot in my sleep. I laugh and tell her she isn't the first to notice this. I receive my dose of Librium and anti-anxiety medication and the nurse connects a fresh Pabrinex bag.

My mum rouses from her sleep and looks at me and smiles. She asks me how I'm feeling and I respond, "Anxious."

Today I'm going to try and go for a cigarette if I feel strong enough. I haven't smoked since I came in and I am itching for a drag.

I am able to stomach some coffee and eat a slice of toast with butter on it. As soon as I swallow the drink I feel it burn in my chest and I like the feeling. The same feeling I used to get when I drank whiskey. That burning feeling makes me feel warm and calm; it hurts but feels good. The food makes me feel sick. I stopped eating for a while before hospital; every time I ate I threw it up so I became very anxious about ingesting any food.

I keep the food down, and I turn on the TV.

Frasier is on, a show that reminds me of being thirteen and waking up for my paper round. It was always so early that these re-runs were all I would watch before heading out.

It's hard to write about the daytime events of being in hospital. Not much happens, I suppose.

My back is aching from the damage I've inflicted on myself with alcohol, and I am always tired. The rest of my family turn up and sit with me while I lie in my bed. I tell them about all the strange things I'm seeing and feel like it won't go, like I'm stuck in this nightmare forever.

They tell me how proud of me they are and how well I'm doing, and to look forward to my life without pain when I leave.

I feel so lucky to have such wonderful people around me. My sister and I have never really got on, and she's been amazing since I've been ill. They leave when it gets dark, but my mum stays, as she always has done.

I want a cigarette; I want a cigarette so badly that the thought of it makes my heart race, like water to a stranded person in a desert. I ask my mum to help me get to the smoking area. She is very wary of me smoking but can see I want it very much.

On the way down to the smoking area, things start happening.

I have been in my room for a couple of days now so I haven't seen much apart from the four walls I've been laying in.

I see people. So many different people. Some walking, some talking, some standing, staring into space, clutching the wall they lean upon. I feel calm, I don't feel scared like I have done before. I feel at peace. Like this is okay, like I shouldn't be seeing this but it's okay that I am.

These people aren't dark figures, they aren't threatening. They are lost, every single one of them. They have the same silver outline in their features as the others, but I can see them much more clearly.

I know no one else can see what I can see. I walk down the steps towards the main corridor and an old woman, frail, looking sad and confused, grips the wall on her own, as if not knowing where to go.

I walk by her and I give her an acknowledging smile and say hello.

She mutters something I can't hear, again, like a whisper. She stares up at me, eyes electric, and cries. She is smiling, and cries as if in appreciation. As though no one has seen her in years. Her hand raises in a subtle wave as I continue down the stairs.

We reach the corridor and I walk down, slowly. Taking in everything that I am seeing.

This feels different. This doesn't feel like the hallucinations I've been seeing, this just feels comforting and incredible.

They walk past me, staring. Standing and staring. Some whispering to each other, whilst looking at me with wide eyes. I nod, I wave, and I acknowledge their stares.

I tell my mum what I am seeing. I tell her this is amazing, this is something that I have never in my life witnessed before and I feel so strange.

A figure is walking down the corridor towards me, very fast and looking agitated.

He is a tall, well dressed Black man. He is wearing clothes that look relatively modern, and a cap. He approaches me, walking fast, speaking under his breath. Panicked words escape, I can't make them out but they are said angrily and quick. He holds my stare as he walks inches from my face, I nod again.

"*He can see us!*"

It scares me, the volume of the shout and the instant turning of heads.

"*He can see us! He can see us!*" The man is screaming this out, over and over behind me as I walk.

As I approach the end of the corridor, the people are turning and approaching me, trying to speak but their words are lost in the whisper.

They are now following me.

I ask my mum if she can see or hear anything; she tells me she can't, obviously.

I walk outside and light my cigarette. The feeling of smoke hitting the back of my throat feels so good. I stand there and feel the rush of light-headedness fill my vision. I stand, shaking. Feeling the relief of the nicotine.

I perch down, leaning against the wall of the smoking area and shut my eyes.

I can hear the whispering still. I turn to my right and see a middle-aged woman, sat down on the wall cradling her arms.

She is like the others. She looks at me with such sadness in her eyes. I approach her and I ask her what the matter is.

She is in such sadness and it's like I can feel it, as if it's coming from her. She whispers something through tears.

I bend down and I try to listen. It's too loud out here to hear anything. My mum tells me people are staring. I stop trying to listen and try to touch her back, to give some comfort. When I stretch out my hand the figure of the woman dissipates and warps.

She comes back into view and stands up, still cradling her arms.

I tell my mum I'm ready to go back upstairs. We begin walking and I notice she is following me, the woman on the wall.

The others inside the hospital seem to notice her following me and allow space for her steps.

I am up the stairs now and she is still behind me.

We arrive in my room. I lay down. I see the figure of the woman walk into my room, and cautiously sit down on the chair next to my bed.

She sits cradling her arms, and I look to see what is there. There is a bundle. I never see the face of what is inside the bundle. But it seems to be a baby. She is crying, inconsolable, tears like drops of blue ice falling from her fluorescent eyes.

I ask her to tell me why she is crying. I feel her pain and it is choking me.

She reaches out and rests her hand on mine.

I feel immediate cold on my skin. Like a glove that's been sitting in the freezer has just been placed on my hand.

I feel the same feeling I did with Super Alex in my room.

I am not in my room anymore. I am in an older hospital, what feels like mid-nineties; a woman is lying in bed, scared, alone.

She is shaking, she has no one there for her and she is terrified. She cradles a baby in her arms and cries out. She screams and shouts, pleading with whoever will listen.

Blood soaks the bed beneath her legs and doctors rush around her and take the baby from her arms.

She writhes in desperation and cries out for her baby. Doctors hold her, trying to calm her down, telling her they need to operate, she has lost too much blood.

The baby has not survived. She fades into a blur, the doctors and the hospital room fade from view and I am back in my bed, cold hand placed on mine, tears in my eyes.

I have seen her pain; somehow I have witnessed her last moments. She nods her head, smiling through tears. I feel such empathy, such pain.

She gets up, stands by my bed for a minute or two and slowly, backs out of the room.

She's gone.

Whatever I am seeing, I am told it isn't real, which of course I understand. But it is real to me. I am left emotional and filled with questions.

I cry in my bed and explain to my mum what I have witnessed; she comforts me and tells me to rest.

I shut my eyes and wait for sleep to come.

Morning comes around like an unwelcome guest. The familiar shaking and sweating have come back; I ride it out and try to watch some TV.

My nurse appears in my room, gives me my meds and leaves. The shaking begins to subside and I lay back and try to relax. Today, my friend Isaac is coming to see me. Isaac has been my best friend since I was young. He is a musician in a very talented punk band from my area and has had a lot of success in this. We don't see as much as each other as we both would like, but it feels like no time has passed when we greet each other.

I am so elated that he is here. I am sorry he has to see me in such a way, but beyond grateful for the visit. He sits down next to my bed, my mum sitting also in the room, and we catch up.

I tell him how I have been seeing hallucinations. I explain excitedly about Super Alex, and how I have been seeing what feel like ghosts. He smiles and tells me how mental that must be, to see such things. I agree and we both laugh.

My mum is explaining to Isaac what has been happening, as I don't think my state of mind is granting me much sanity in this moment. I am still hallucinating, but not to a degree that it is scaring me.

I tell my friend I love him, and I appreciate his visit. He smiles and says how good it is to see me doing better.

My mum takes a picture of us, just so I can look back on it when I'm better.

We say our goodbyes and he leaves.

I feel so much love from my friends and family. I feel so lucky.

The weather outside is starting to open up. Mist is dissipating giving way to beams of sunlight, streaming across my bed. It feels warm, I feel safe.

My doctor strides into my room, a nurse on his tail, talking fast and checking my chart.

He is a tall man, dark skin, dark hair and glasses. He approaches me and I realise this is really the first time I have properly met him.

On every other occasion I have been extremely doped up or just unable to focus on anything but the strange things I am seeing.

"How are we feeling, Mr. Mackey?" He looks up from my chart that he has retrieved from the foot of my bed, eyebrows raised.

I look back at him vulnerable and anxious.

"Fine, getting better I think. Still shaking and sweating, keep seeing things still."

"Yes well, it's been a tough few days for you so far. You have been very lucky to have such a supportive family around you, your mother hasn't left your side…"

He looks at my mum with a smile; she smiles back gratefully.

"Are you still having visual hallucinations? The nurses say you have been a lot calmer than when we first had you in here."

The nurse nods and smiles in agreement.

"I am still seeing things, mostly in the corner of my eyes, but yesterday was worse. I saw what felt like ghosts in the halls of the hospital. One even followed me back to my room…"

He raises his eyebrows again, this time sceptical and dismissive.

"Well yes, the alcohol withdrawal has been in an acute stage for a number of days. You have been receiving vitamins in the form of the Pabrinex drip, and the Librium has been doing its job so these hallucinations should subside any time now."

"I am still shaking quite a lot, will this go completely as well?"

"Yes, this will go too, as will the sweating. Have you been eating? How is your appetite?"

He studies the chart.

"I have managed to eat, yes. It feels very strange to be able to eat properly. But I'm glad I can."

He looks up and places my chart back on my bed.

"Good, that's good. We are looking at discharging you in a couple of days, Depending on how you are coming along. The way things are looking at the moment, two days' time seems probable."

I look at my mum and I smile.

"Okay, thank you so much. You guys have literally saved my life. I can't thank you enough."

"Yes really, thank you," my mum says, standing up and shaking the doctor's hand.

"That's quite all right," he says, smiling appreciatively. "Just stay off the alcohol and hopefully we won't meet again."

"I will, thank you," I say as he exits the room, the nurse following frantically behind.

I turn to my mum and smile. I still have a feeling inside me that I want to drink. Even after all of this, I don't want to stop forever. Day to day life isn't exciting or fun. I feel I have taken it too far but now I feel better and that I can control it. I mention this to my mum; she says maybe non-alcoholic beers but not alcohol. She looks at me deeply worried, as if she already knows I'm going to drink again.

The terrifying thing is that even after this, all these things I've seen and how lucky I am to get better, there is still part of me inside that just wants to be normal like everyone else. I'm young, I'm too young to be not drinking when that is literally all everyone does when they go out. I am already planning; I'm still in bed recovering and already I'm plotting my next drink.

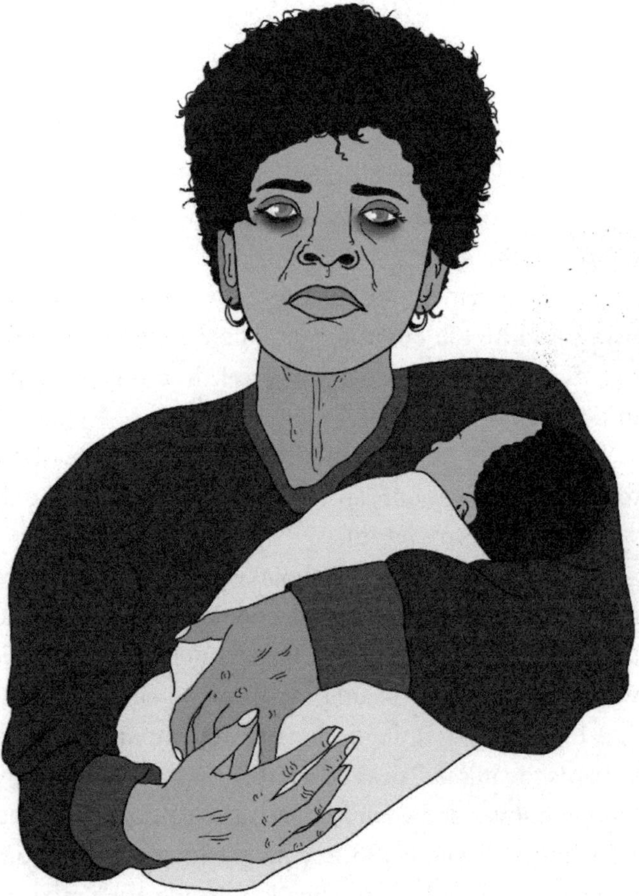

Chapter 4: Leaving

It's the day I'm being discharged. I am feeling better, not a hundred percent but a hell of a lot better than when I walked into hospital. My mum and my sister are here to take me home.

I am extremely nervous. I feel very anxious about being back in the environment where I witnessed such horrific hallucinations, and where I, in a way, lost my mind.

I think my mum knows this. She has tried her best to change my room around at home and make it welcoming for my return.

I have thought a lot about drinking again. I am going to try to just drink non-alcoholic beers etcetera, to try and see if that helps. I have a horrible feeling it won't, but I am also scared I will end up back here.

I gather my things up with my mum and head towards the nurses' desk to get discharged. They all say their goodbyes and wish me well, and all are very sweet. I am taken through too a separate room where I am given a bag full of my medication. Inside are a mixture of beta blockers and vitamins that I will have to take for my anxiety and to get my body back to feeling strong and healthy again.

No one has really explained to me what the protocol is now. How susceptible am I to this happening again? Will I be able to drink normally from now on? Will I become addicted to alcohol like before or now I am better will I be able to drink like a normal person? So many questions I never ask.

I take my new medication with me as I walk out the door and head towards the staircase leading to the lower corridor. The same corridor that not two days ago was bustling with ghostly figures, staring at me, looking lost and confused.

I feel strangely alone now they are not here; there was a feeling of comfort when I could see them, and now that has gone.

My family is excited for me; they talk to me of all the opportunities I will have now. Of how I can do anything I want to do. Apart from the *one* thing I want to.

I feel like my brain is the problem. There is something deeply wrong inside. Something that is never satisfied, a thirst that is never quenched, that gnaws at my sanity. The more I try to think of something else, the bigger the feeling becomes inside. Like attempting to quiet the feeling makes the obsession worse.

I don't even realise we have reached the car.

I feel the familiar leather on my skin. I sat here five days ago, in a very different state of mind. I feel anxiety seeping into my gut. I feel nauseous; every move of the car is too much. I want to be still. I feel things are moving too quick for me to keep up. I am starting to realise that I cannot drink when I return home. This feeling makes me scared and confused.

We pull up to our house, and park in the driveway. My mum turns to me and smiles.

"New start, Jacko."

I smile back nervously.

"Yup."

Chapter 5: Hiding in plain sight

I wake up from possibly one of the best night's sleep I have ever had.

The same bed that I became so used to yielding nothing but sleeplessness and irritation was now a haven. I lay staring up at the ceiling collecting my thoughts, daydreaming into the canvas of white plaster. I stretch out and turn to my phone to check my messages.

Two messages.

One from my gran asking how I slept after my first night home, and another from my friend Isaac asking me if I would like to go to his house for dinner that week.

The messages make me smile. I jump off my bed, feeling very lucky and happy to have people in my life like them.

My brother is downstairs having breakfast. I walk into the kitchen and say good morning. He approaches me and gives me a tight hug.

"Missed you, buddy," he says mid hug.

"Missed you too, man," I say, releasing him and leaning against the kitchen counter.

I flip on the kettle and stand patiently waiting for its familiar bubbling.

We catch up as I wait, asking him how school is, whether anything has happened while I have been in hospital and just talking in general about how fucked up the whole experience was. He tells me he is proud of me and that he is glad that I am doing better and walks out of the room and heads upstairs.

I put four teaspoons of coffee in a large mug and hold my face up to the brim. I inhale the rich aroma and close my eyes. It smells great.

I pour the boiling water into the mug and take a long drink.

The burning feeling reminds me of the warm sensation alcohol would make hitting my stomach. I always loved that feeling.

I roll a cigarette and head outside.

As quickly as the happiness came, emptiness fills me. This isn't a surprise as I am often feeling happy and sad moments apart; no one has been able to explain why that is to me yet.

I feel so lost. I am happy that I survived such a mad experience, but I am not ready to think too hard about it. I smoke my cigarette and lose myself in a daydream.

The next few days come and go, I go to my friend's house and I have dinner with his family, all of them are extremely supportive and make me feel even luckier that I have such people in my life.

It is still there though. I still want a drink. I still want to feel nothing. I go home and go to sleep, trying to silence the cravings in my head.

I get a message from my friend asking me if I would like to come and watch him perform in London at a very large, well-known venue. I say yes immediately. His band is a two-piece punk band and they have found success with their debut album recently released.

I tell my mum and she looks worried.

"What about drinking, won't there be drinking there?"

I think about this for a second.

"There will be but I will drink non-alcoholic beers there, I won't drink anything else"

She looks at me extremely worried. I assure her I won't drink.

The day comes around and I am given a lift up there with a few other friends and I drink non-alcoholic beers in the car ride up.

I catch up with a few of the guys in the car with me. I have known them for a while and they ask me countless questions about hospital, whether or not I can drink again – to this I answer I can, but not to the degree I was – and how I am doing now. I lie and tell them I am fine. Honestly, I am anything but fine. I am shitting myself. Being in this environment so soon I feel is really throwing me and not drinking feels completely unnatural.

Why did I lie when they asked me if I can drink again? I mean I don't know the rules, but I'm pretty sure that the advice from the doctor would be firmly not to drink again. I mean, maybe I can drink? Maybe I can have a few, get drunk and then not wake up and drink. Maybe things can go back to normal?

The guys are talking and I am just staring out of the car window, asking myself these questions and filling my head with maybes.

We arrive and it is really busy. The air is thick with mist and the murmur of people in the distance queuing for the gig brings a jolt of adrenaline through my veins. I hope we don't have to queue.

We obviously do end up queuing and I find it difficult being around so many people. I am sober; the non-alcoholic drinks are doing absolutely nothing, and I am anxious and awkward.

I go on my phone and pretend to text. I always find this helps take my mind off where I am when I am overwhelmed. The queue begins to move and we reach the door. There is an attractive tattooed woman with a headset sitting at a desk with two others next to her taking tickets. Two large looking gentlemen standing behind her are checking people's bags.

I give my name. She motions that she can't hear me.

I lean over and say my name into her ear. She acknowledges this and checks the list. My name is there and she stamps my forearm so I can enter.

We go into the venue and it is huge. The hall we walk into is staggering. Ceilings that feel like they're a mile high and what feels like thousands of people bustling about excitedly.

I want to stand near the back. I love my friend but I am claustrophobic and the thought of being jammed between others, sweating and jumping around, is my idea of a nightmare. I stand at the back on my own.

I see the bar. My friends see the bar. They motion for me to come with them and I follow.

I order myself another zero percent and take a long swig of it. It tastes like dirt.

I feel like an idiot. I feel like I'm wounded and every single person in the room knows it because I'm not drinking. I start to seriously consider having a cider.

My friend's band comes on and they are amazing. I guess I've been so wrapped up in my own stuff for so long and haven't been to see them since they started out. The music is loud and the vibrations ricochet throughout my body. I stand at the bar the whole gig, as I feel like I'm safe there. Far away from the moshing fans and in my own secure bubble.

I know I should be enjoying myself more. I know I should be like my old self and be the life and soul of the party and get involved with smashing into others, drunk and carefree, going mental to the music.

I turn to the ba tender.

"Do you have cider?" I shout over the music.

"Yeah, what do you want?

"Your cheapest!" I say, jokingly, but very much meaning it.

The bartender pulls me a pint of ice cold cider and places it on the side.

I am almost expecting him to say I can't have it. To say, "Ah, hang on, you're not meant to be drinking, are you, Jack?" and for me to cower away in humiliation.

I am on my own in this. My friends are busy having a good time, and I am stood alone with my pint of crazy juice.

I pay, I pick up, and I sink it.

Jesus.

That warm feeling is back. That tingling in my stomach. That smile inducing euphoria is here and I fucking love it. I order two more pints before I have even finished the first.

I stand against the bar, I shut my eyes and I stay with that feeling. I realise I am shaking. Not through withdrawal, but through pure excitement. This is forbidden fruit, this is wrong, so wrong but feels so fucking right.

I am smiling, I am happy. I drink all three pints in the space of five minutes and head out of the hall for a cigarette.

I am not thinking right now. I'm not thinking of the repercussions of the move I just made. I am not thinking of the past weeks that were the worst of my life, I am just not thinking, and it feels fantastic.

I reach the top of some stairs outside the venue and I spark my cigarette. Jesus, even smoking feels so much better. I stand, swaying slightly, taking in drags and staring off into the distance.

I am finding myself already coming up with excuses and easy rational reasons why it will be fine this time.

'I just won't drink in the mornings this time. That's it! As long as I keep it to just weekends and make sure I'm eating well, it'll be fine. I can do that! It was that way before things got bad so things can be that easy again.'

I now don't feel guilty or bad about the move I have made. I feel calm, I feel normal, finally.

I head back inside and I go back to the bar.

I order a shot of whiskey and another pint of cider. One of my friends spots me and comes over, out of breath and red faced.

"Where were you, man! We were all in the mosh pit," he says, panting.

"That's not my kind of thing, dude, I just feel relaxed over here."

He looks down at the drink in my hand and raises his eyebrows.

"Should you really be... I thought you couldn't..."

"They just said if I don't do what I did before then I can drink normally."

He looks concerned but shrugs and comes and joins me leaning on the bar.

I have been drinking for around half an hour and I've already started to lie. When I lie I don't feel bad, if anything it makes me feel safer in what I'm doing. I feel it's just easier to tell a truth that I want to hear.

My friend's band is finishing their set with a fan favourite and the audience is going crazy. Everybody is singing along and the set is ending with a bang. I polish off my drinks and order another.

We head to the backstage area, which is down some stairs next to the stage. There is security on the door and everything is very official. We reach the bottom of the stairs and the floor opens up into a large room with a bar, sofas and music.

It feels like a trendy nightclub really. I look around for my friend to congratulate him on his set, and as I am scanning the room I notice more than a few famous musicians.

It's very exciting to be in a room where some of the people who inspired me to pick up an instrument are standing around chatting. I have never experienced being starstruck before, but this must be it.

I find my friend and go over to him and congratulate him on his performance. He thanks me and we hug. He asks how I am and almost immediately spots the drink I'm holding.

He came and visited me in hospital, and knows how bad things were, so to say he looks concerned is an understatement.

"Mate, should you be drinking?"

I go red, embarrassed. He doesn't mean to embarrass me and no one is near us to overhear the conversation.

"I know, man, I shouldn't really, the doctor said as long as I don't go as mad and heavy as before I should be okay, plus this is my first drink."

Lie after lie after lie. I am already lying to my best friend, but again, it's easier than admitting the truth. This is neither the time nor place for me to get into it.

"Okay, brother," he says cautiously and hugs me again. "I only say it because I care, mate. I'm glad you came!" I agree and say how wonderful it was to watch him play.

We stay at the bar for a while. I have a good time catching up with people I haven't seen in a while and feel like a normal person for the first time in a long time.

I lose track of how many drinks I have had. I know it's a lot.

We leave around midnight and start driving back. On the way home I drink in the car. I also stop off at a garage to pick up a bottle of wine and some cans of cider for when I get home.

We laugh and sing along to music in the car and I am dropped off outside my house.

I wave goodbye to my friends and thank them for taking me to and from the gig.

I didn't think about this part. This is where it does matter that I'm drinking. If my mum sees me drunk she will be devastated. I bunch up the bottle and cans together in the plastic bag to stop them knocking together and making noise. I place them on the floor and lift the pot outside my front door looking for the key.

I find it and enter the house. I have a strong feeling of guilt overwhelming me. I want another drink. I head into the front room of our house and I fill up a pint glass with white wine. I drain the glass and switch on the TV. I drink and I watch. I shut my eyes. I sleep.

I wake up early morning. My head is splitting, mouth is dry and anxiety pulses through my body. I am still in the living room of my house and I have wine soaked into my shirt. I am shaking violently as I try to stand up.

I try not to panic. I try to focus on rolling a cigarette and keeping my breathing steady. I keep telling myself I can't be withdrawing; surely this can't happen? I left hospital not long ago and I was fixed. Isn't my body back to normal?

Before I can even make it to the toilet I am sick violently, clasping my hand over my mouth to try and stop it but it just keeps coming. I make it to the toilet and I throw my head into its cold interior. I am loudly vomiting and I hear my mum rush downstairs.

"Oh my god, Jack…"

I feel the hurt in her voice.

"Oh my god, you said you weren't going to drink!"

I cannot reply. I am gasping for air between heaving violently, retching so hard I experience what feels like my chest muscles ripping. I manage to catch my breath and I wail hard. I cry and I say, "I'm sorry, I'm so sorry, Mum."

She kneels next to me and rubs my back, fighting back tears of her own.

"This is it, no more, Jack, you are going to end up back in hospital."

I cry and I reach over my shoulder for her hand and I hold it tight.

"I don't know why I can't stop, Mum," I say breathlessly. "Something inside me is broken, I can't fight it, there is something wrong with me, and I don't know what to do."

I cry hard. I cry like a child. My mum, as she has always been, is by my side comforting me. She tells me it will be okay, I just need to stop. I need to stop now.

"I can't, Mum, I just feel like I can't stop."

"You *can*, Jack!" she yells, gripping my hand tighter. "You know you can! You just need to want it."

I lift my body up against the porcelain base and rest on the wall to regain my balance. I turn to my mum and I hug her tight. She tells me to go and lie down and I proceed to my room and collapse onto the bed. My head is thumping, my hands are shaking, the world is spinning.

Feelings of regret and shame are overwhelming me, consuming my thoughts. How could I have been so stupid? Why couldn't I have said no like a normal person? No one forced me to drink, I did that myself.

I am panicking and can't rest. I sit up and search the room. I see a bottle of wine in a plastic bag next to my bed and before I have time to process what I am doing, I drink.

It tastes like acid in my mouth. I push through and drain half of it. I watch my hands. I wait patiently for the shaking to subside.

Nothing yet.

I drain more and I shut my eyes and wait. The warm feeling is spreading through my body. Starting at the pit of my stomach, traveling to my fingers and my toes. I inhale and exhale deeply. I look at my hands. The shaking is subsiding. I feel euphoria sweep through my mind and no longer feel panicked.

The feeling is something I can't describe. When you experience withdrawal from alcohol it can come in many forms. I know from experience that my withdrawal is always severe. It comes on fast and strong, incapacitating me and filling my whole body with feelings of doom, dread, horror and fear. The urge to get something alcoholic in me is the most overpowering urge; it's primal. It is my comfort blanket, my doctor and my best friend.

I hear the door to my room begin to open and I don't hide the bottle.

"*No!*"

My mum runs towards me and grabs hold of the bottle.

"I need it!" I shout, grasping it in my hands and pulling it towards my chest.

I can feel my mum really trying hard to take it from me, but that isn't going to happen.

"I just watched you almost die in hospital and throw your guts up five minutes ago! Please *stop*!"

I hang on tight to the bottle.

"I'm having really bad withdrawal! I can't stop, Mum!"

She releases her grip; she looks physically and emotionally exhausted.

"Fine, Jack, but I'm not going to help you kill yourself." I feel like I've broken her heart. "Call up CRI today and arrange a meeting to get help, please, it's the least you can do."

(CRI are an alcohol and substance abuse support team that help addicts cut down and quit alcohol in the community.)

I agree to this and tell her I'm sorry. What else can I say?

Chapter 6: Back to square one

I wait in my room. I have already drunk two, two litre bottles of strong cider. It's nine-fifty a.m.

Today I have my appointment with CRI. They help to detox addicts in the community, cut down, stop altogether and generally give help for people like myself.

Last time I came here I didn't like it. I didn't get the answers I wanted. When you don't know about alcoholism or addiction you think it's going to be just 'stop drinking, you'll be fine'. Instead, it's 'cut down slowly because you are at risk of withdrawal' etcetera. Basically it is hard. Hard fucking work. And I don't feel I have the strength to do that.

I'm shaking. I'm fucking scared. I'm fucking anxious. I don't want to leave this house.

What if I am sick in the car? What if I shit myself? What if I have a seizure? What if I have a panic attack?

I down some cider.

Ah, fuck, I need to calm down. My heart won't stop. It's thumping in my chest, so hard I feel it's going to explode.

Keep drinking. Drinking stops this feeling. Keep drinking.

"You ready to go, love?" My mum pops her head into my room, looking stressed.

"Do we have to do this? Why can't they come to me? I'm so scared I'm going to withdraw, Mum."

"You are not going to withdraw, darling. You have drunk more than enough to make your symptoms calm down. They can't just come out to you, Jack, that's not how this works."

"I know, I'm just scared," I say. I'm feeling hot and like I can't breathe.

"It'll be okay, love, that's why we are seeing them, to get you better."

I stand up and put on my Jacket. I grab a bottle of cider from the fridge and place it in a rucksack and head out of the front door.

I open the car door and climb into the front seat. I take out the cider and place it at my feet. As long as this cider is by my feet I will be okay. I won't withdraw, I have my cider here. My mum gets in, puts on her seatbelt, and looks at me and smiles.

We start the journey and I feel the gas and acid in my stomach churning. I have never been able to burp so I stick my fingers down my throat and wretch. As soon as I do this a burning feeling rushes up my throat and I am sick on myself.

"Jack, Jesus Christ! Why the hell did you do that?"

"I don't know…" I moan as I try to wipe off the sick on my jumper. My eyes are streaming and I feel disgusting.

"I'm so sorry, Mum."

I shut my eyes and try to cool myself down by winding down the window.

"It's okay, love, just warn me if you're going—"

"*Pull over!*"

The feeling is back and I know I'm going to be sick I motion to my mum to stop the car and she pulls into a layby and I launch myself out the car. I plunge my head into a bush and empty everything I've consumed this morning. I cry in between breaths. My mum comes over to me and rubs my back.

"Oh, love." I can hear a wavering in her voice.

"I can't believe I've done this to myself again, I can't stand being alive, Mum, and I hate this," I cry, struggling to breathe through stomach spasms and tears.

"I know, Jacko, I know it's hard but we will get you better," she says.

"What if I can't get better?" The anxiety is coming back. I'm shaking now.

"Can't isn't an option, love, you will and I'm here for you."

I straighten up and hug her. We get in the car and I try to roll a cigarette.

Hands are shaking, need a drink. I lift the bottle and down a quarter of it.

It's warm in my stomach, the warmth spreads and seems to calm down my heart. I continue to roll the cigarette.

We arrive in at CRI. The journey is usually not longer than fifteen minutes; we are a couple of minutes late. We pull in behind what looks like a row of shops and park up in a dilapidated car park. My mum tells me I can't bring my cider in with me so I drink as much of it as I can until I feel I can't stomach anymore.

She links my arm as she can see I'm not a hundred percent on my feet. We walk to the entrance, press the buzzer and ascend into what looks like an office floor. I approach the front desk with my mum and she speaks for me.

"Hello! Jack Mackey? We have an appointment for ten-thirty with Tracey?"

The receptionist smiles. "Okay! Let me just have a look." She scans the computer. "Yup, that's fine, if you can just take a seat over there and she will be with you shortly."

We walk over to a set of cushioned chairs set against a wall. My mum nudges me, smiles and points at the wall in front of us.

YOUR LIFE MAY NOT BE WORKING OUT THE WAY YOU PLANNED BUT THAT IS NOT AN EXCUSE TO JUST GIVE UP. MAKE THE MOST OF TODAY, AND YOU MIGHT BE SURPRISED WHERE YOU END UP TOMORROW.

The words printed on the wall hit me cynically. I raise my eyebrows back at my mum in a 'yeah, yeah' sort of way. If a saying was going to help me, it would be very fucking easy.

A small middle-aged woman walks briskly towards us. She has red hair, glasses and, most importantly, a warm, kind smile on her face which immediately puts me in a calm state.

If I'm honest, when I have been here before, the key workers I have had haven't helped me at all. My last key worker was a man who was incredibly lovely but had a very 'tough love' approach to me cutting down and stopping drinking. The facts weren't clear to me or my family, and it didn't work out. I don't think I react well at all to 'tough love'; I see it as attacking me and I fight against it. I think that having a good key worker is a lot like having a good therapist; if they are right for you, you just know it and it clicks. Let's be clear, I've been here three times before for three separate attempts at stopping/cutting down and it didn't take, so I am highly sceptical.

"'Ello there! You must be Jack! And this is your mum, I'm guessin'?" She shakes my hand enthusiastically and proceeds to do the same to my mum. She has a midlands accent, sounds Brummie, I think. I'm not entirely sure but it's a nice accent.

"Hello," I say. " Nice to meet you."

"He's polite, isn't he, your lad?" she says, still smiling at my mum.

My mum smiles, in a very thankful way. "At times…" she says, smiling at me and winking.

"Ooh really?" says Tracey, smiling and beckoning us to follow her into a small room.

We sit down and I look at my mum. She seems hopeful which gives me hope.

Tracey sits down and she starts sifting through a file and then proceeds to clap her hands together and address me and my mum.

"OK, so, Jack, tell me what's been happening"

"Okay, um, basically er…" My mind has gone blank, why now? I can't think. I'm so anxious I can't seem to get any words out. I'm sweating and shaking and feeling like I want to burst into tears.

"Mum, can you explain? I'm sorry I'm feeling so anxious and can't think."

I feel fucking useless. I can't even tell the person who can help me what's wrong. I've always struggled with my anxiety, but since drinking it's got so much worse.

"Okay, love, it's okay," she says, patting my hand.

My mum proceeds to tell Tracey about everything that has been happening, the hospital, the relapse back into drinking at the gig, the speed at which I seem to have withdrawals, the depression and the amount I've been drinking.

"It's only been a few days since he started drinking again but it seems he's right back to where he started. He is terrified at night because he doesn't want to be alone in case he hallucinates and I just don't know what else to do."

Tracey looks at me with a very warm, understanding smile. I think I may cry.

"I just feel that I won't be able to stop drinking at home. I'm so scared every day and I just want it all to stop." I'm talking but as I speak I feel the tears coming. I start to sob into my hands. I can't stop it. I'm so tired of all of this. I just want it to end. I can't keep letting my family down. I want to die.

My mum puts her hand on my back and Tracey holds my arm.

"We will get you better, Jack, you're not alone in this. I know you're upset and feel at the end of your rope but your mum is behind you and so am I."

I nod through tears and try to smile.

"I think it's clear you aren't able to cut down alcohol in an outpatient capacity," she says. "So what I'm going to do is put you forward for inpatient detox in Maidstone."

She clicks onto her computer and pulls up some information on the detox facility.

"What does that mean? Is that like what they did in hospital to get me better?" I say. My heart is pounding.

"It's very similar, but this place is more for getting you the help you need. The hospital help you get better physically, but this place helps mentally and physically. Plus they help you come off alcohol in a controlled environment, with twenty-four hour staff to take care of you."

My mum is crying now.

"We have been told about this before but nothing has happened. I just don't want us to get our hopes up and then nothing comes of it." My mum is sceptical because we have been informed about this before and then never heard anything again about it.

"No, I understand that, but it's clear Jack isn't well at all and he clearly isn't able to do outpatient detox."

"Oh, thank god, that would be amazing, wouldn't it, Jack?" My mum holds my hand and looks at my hopefully.

"Absolutely," I say. And I mean it. If I can go to this place, it will save my life. Tracey will save my life.

I cry and thank Tracey.

"When would this happen?" I am, in all honesty, terrified of dying before I get the chance to get better.

"I have to put your case forward to the higher ups, but I will push very hard to get this done quickly. There is a waiting list to get into places like this, but I will do my best to get you up the list because you are in such a bad way."

"Thank you so much, I can't tell you what this means to me." Me and my mum are smiling at each other. I finally feel I have hope.

I realise we haven't mentioned my diet as of yet.

"Also I haven't been able to eat much at all, and when I do eat, I either throw it up very quickly or I feel so exhausted and my anxiety becomes unbearable."

"Right, that is most likely because your body is working extra hard to digest what you are eating. I would recommend eating small amounts, as often as you can. I will also recommend you get some vitamin replacement tablets as you're losing essential vitamins because of the lack of food and water."

"Okay, we can do that," my mum says.

"I feel like I'm withdrawing now," I say. My hands have begun shaking violently, I'm sweating through my jumper and have begun to feel numb in my fingertips.

"Okay, have you got alcohol with you?" she says.

"Yes, in the car."

"Okay, well I just need to give you some information about what we discussed, two minutes tops, and then I'll let you go and you can sort that out."

"Okay, thank you."

We quickly discuss information regarding the facility, and I am told to try and keep to the amount I'm drinking at the moment. Otherwise I am likely to start hallucinating again and experiencing DTs (delirium tremens).

I shake Tracey's hand, thank her profusely and we leave.

My mum links my arm once again and we descend the stairs. "I can't believe it, Jacko, we didn't expect that result, did we?"

"No, not at all," I respond. "I feel hope, Mum, for the first time in a long time I see a light at the end of the tunnel."

"I know, love, me too" She smiles through tears rolling down her cheeks.

We get in the car and she exhales with relief and we begin our journey home. Things are looking up, I can't believe it, finally.

Chapter 7: Sleepless nights and surreal days

I keep to what Tracey said. I drink what I need to, and I eat what I can. Eating when you are so bodily dependant on alcohol is beyond exhausting. In my mind, food makes me sober again, or starts to soak up my alcohol. So for me to eat is a struggle.

I start out with one slice of toast in the mornings. I say mornings, Right now I am waking up at around 4 o'clock in the morning after about an hour's sleep.

I start to drift off, I feel sleepy, and then my body is jolted awake by a surge of adrenaline, and I'm back to being wide awake again. The only way I can get any sleep at all is to drink enough to hold off my withdrawals and so I'm semi drunk and then I can maybe drift off. I begin drinking as soon as I wake up. My legs shake like a baby deer when I wake up, every time. I have to balance against a wall and my bed to lift myself off the bed. I go downstairs and I pour myself a pint of cider.

I always down the first pint. Always. I just need it inside me. Once it's inside me my legs begin to work again, my arms no longer feel numb and I can slow my heart rate. It usually takes the first three pints until I feel semi normal.

The constant sickness is a nightmare. If I'm not drinking or trying to eat, I'm being sick. Once someone described cider as 'liquid bread' to me because it gives your stomach the feeling of being full, and it is just very filling. That feeling can also give way to such hunger pains and gas that I will spend every half an hour in the toilet being sick.

Obviously, there is hardly anything in my stomach apart from what I've drunk. So what I am throwing up is bile, blood and the alcohol my body needs. It's an endless cycle and a daily hell.

After all of this in the morning, I reach a moment when maybe my stomach is settled enough for the toast. When I eat it, the food sits in my stomach like a foreign object. My body begins to try and reject it, but if I want to survive until I go into the detox facility I must keep it down.

Right now I'm up to around four two litre bottles of cider a day. The acid burns my gums and my throat stings with every drink.

I don't do much with my days at the moment. In all honesty there isn't much I can do.

Things are tense between me and my mum at the moment.

She is quite literally watching her son die in front of her and there's nothing she can do. I am at a point where I am so dependant that if I don't have the amount of alcohol in my body I need, I could die. So the doctors and people at CRI have told us we have to do this. And naturally she is absolutely devastated by this.

My sister Jess has moved into a new flat with her boyfriend Ben. I have said that I will go up to see her with my younger brother. Obviously, this has to be meticulously planned for me, as If I don't have the necessary alcohol I need throughout the day I can withdraw. The last thing I need is to be stuck in London withdrawing.

I and my sister have had a very strange and turbulent relationship growing up. To be honest I was a nightmare to be around. She had her own stuff going on and I was always very difficult to live with when young.

I have always had extremely bad temper issues. Something me and my family have tried and failed to have diagnosed and fixed, but no one could ever give us answers. As I grew older, it became a little easier to deal with my anger, but it was still there. We have tried slowly to rebuild our relationship. It's getting there but not fully healed and I don't think it will be for a while. I just want to show her I care about her and I'm sorry for how I've acted in the past, especially now. She has been an incredible support to me and my mum throughout my addiction, so going up to see her is something I very much want to do.

I speak to my brother about the day we are going to see her and what we are going to be doing. He mentions that they were thinking of going to the Natural History

Museum. I love history, always have, but this scares me. Can I even bring my drink into this place? He tells me he isn't sure but I decide I'm going to bring a rucksack with me with my alcohol inside it. Also I will bring a sports bottle with me so I can drink it without being noticed.

My stomach has been getting worse recently. I will have to take a lot of Imodium before we go up there as honestly with the way I am at the moment, risks are high for me having an accident.

I can't believe I have to think about this if, I'm honest. I'm twenty-two, I'm not ninety years old, but the way my body feels I may as well be.

The day comes around and me and my brother Ben get a lift to the station and board our train.

In my bag I have eight cans of cider and a packet of Imodium. I began drinking as usual around four o'clock that morning so I am not withdrawing. I am anxious to be on a train and around everyday people, but I am determined to do this. Not just for my sister but also for myself. Ever since this all started I haven't felt normal. I want one fucking day to be normal, one day to spend time with my brother and sister and bring some joy into my dark repetitive life I'm living.

It's the weekend, so in all honesty it doesn't look that bizarre for two lads being on a train to London drinking (albeit only one of them), so I don't feel too self-conscious.

My brother is a great guy. He is six years younger than me, very sporty and a bright, funny character. Unfortunately, he has had to be around me drinking at home for quite a while. He, like me, is a very sensitive person. At home there have been many times he has been sad or upset by my actions with drinking; also to that measure he has been a great wonderful support through this.

"How you feeling, buddy?" he asks me, smiling.

"I'm feeling okay, bit nervous but glad I'm coming to see Jess with you."

"Me too, mate. If you feel overwhelmed at any point let me know and if there's anything I can do."

"Thanks, man, means a lot."

"No problem, bro!"

We reach London Bridge and get on a tube to head towards Kensington. It's busy, hot and stuffy as we board the train. I shut my eyes when we sit down and I try to think of something to calm my nerves. I think Ben knows I'm getting anxious as he asks me if I'm okay. I tell him I'm fine, just feeling claustrophobic.

I reach down to my bag and open a can of cider. I hide it under my Jacket. Not that I need to, but I don't want my brother to feel embarrassed.

"What are you doing?" he says, smiling.

"I didn't want to embarrass you," I say.

"Don't be silly, mate, nobody cares if you drink, mate. It's not illegal! Plus I'm not embarrassed."

I smile at him gratefully, but still hide it under my Jacket. It's sweet of him to make me feel better.

We arrive and exit the station and my sister is waiting for us just outside. I forgot how much I love London. For me there is always a feeling that anything is possible when I'm here, it's literally one of the capitals of the world for music, fashion, everything. I smile and wave at my sister and approach and give her a hug.

"Hey! How was your journey?"

"Yeah, it was okay," I say smiling.

Jess gives Ben a hug and speaks to him while I smoke a cigarette. I am once again very anxious. I have my can of cider sitting open in my coat pocket. I remove it and drink as much of it as I can before we head to the museum. Jess comes over and asks if I'm ready to head off, and I say yes.

We walk towards and the museum and I feel nervous. I ask my sister if it's okay that I have drink in my bag; she doesn't think it'll be an issue. As soon as we get there, a man is checking bags at the entrance. Just my fucking luck. I hand mine over and to my surprise he doesn't even seem to care about the alcohol.

"Is that okay?" I say nervously.

"Yes, fine, thank you, just make sure you don't drink it in there."

I'm going to drink it in there, I have to, but he doesn't need to know that.

I used to come here when I was younger with my sister and brother on day visits with my mum. I always loved looking at the dinosaur models and wonder how they managed to find out what they looked like. It was like magic to me.

We start looking around the exhibits. My nerves have calmed down now, but I still excuse myself to the toilet to have a drink. I go into a cubicle and down two cans of cider very fast. I'm sick into the toilet. I straighten up, walk out to the sink and wash my face.

"Are you okay?" says an old man to my right, washing his hands.

"Oh god, I'm sorry, yes, I'm fine thank you for asking though," I say, feeling incredibly embarrassed and blushing.

His smile drops as he notices the empty can of cider poking out of my bag. He finishes washing his hands and exits the toilet quickly. I feel mortified. I try to forget it as I leave the toilet; the truth is this sort of thing happens quite regularly for me, it doesn't exactly shock me anymore. When people see a person drinking in a place they 'shouldn't be', they usually assume they have a character flaw, as this is the society we live in. I mean I can't really blame them, not everyone you meet who is drinking in a public place is a struggling alcoholic, but the embarrassment never gets easier.

We head towards an exhibition about mammals and there is a massive blue whale on the ceiling, hanging, covering most of the impressive hall we are standing in.

"Fuck me…" I blurt out.

My brother laughs.

"Big innit…" I say.

"Yeah I think that's what David Attenborough said as well, Jack."

We all laugh.

"It is though! I'd shit myself if that popped up underneath me in the sea."

"It'd probably think you were its calf," says my brother.

I laugh loudly and we walk on.

We find an animal model that I find looks similar to me. It has a large snout and is quite chubby. I stand while my sister takes a picture of me next to it, pulling a face that makes me seem like its distant descendant. I have a large nose. Haven't always really but it seems the older I get the more it doesn't want to stop getting in the way, and it most likely still growing. Anyway.

It is so lovely doing this with my brother and sister. We don't spend as much time together as I would like. It's not like I'm begging them to hang out more though, I'm constantly drunk or ill so I'm hardly the easiest person to link up with.

I'm starting to feel a little rough and luckily we decide to leave. I've very much enjoyed today, I am starting to feel ropey though as I haven't had a drink in around an hour. At this point it's after midday so I don't feel guilty about drinking in public. When we leave I open a can and neck it. I immediately feel better. It's probably part psychosomatic but I don't care, I've had my medicine and now I feel better.

We head towards the tube station and begin our journey back to my sister's house. All in all I'm pretty happy with how the day went. I have actually been able to be in public without losing my shit, soiling myself or withdrawing. Ridiculous things to worry about, I know, but to me these are genuinely terrifying things that send me into a panic.

We are on the tube for around twenty minutes and we arrive at my sister's flat. It's a lovely second floor, cosy place. She asks if we would like a drink and I ask if I can put my cider into a glass; she says I can.

Me and my brother sit down in her living room and put on the TV.

"Here you go, bud." My sister enters and puts a glass down in front of me.

"Ah, thank you. Will be nice to actually drink out of a glass rather than a can," I say.

"Yeah, how is the drinking going? I remember last we spoke you said you were having trouble eating?" She looks at me, concerned.

"Still pretty bad. Every time I eat I feel exhausted and anxious, like straight away. It's like my brain starts to freak out because food, in my mind, sobers you up."

"Yeah, that sounds like your anxiety making you think like that," she says.

"Yeah I know, it feels that way."

"You reckon you can eat tonight? I can make some food and if you want any you can have some but if not it's no problem at all, it's here if you want it basically."

This makes me smile. There is nothing worse than feeling food is being forced on me when I feel the way I do. If I know it's there, I can maybe pick at it or eat a small amount if I get hungry at all. There is no pressure, which takes away the anxiety. I pour my cider and start to drink and for the first time in the entire day I actually enjoy it. I don't feel I'm being watched or judged. Although there is a constant feeling of guilt and terror there about the fact I have to drink to stop withdrawal, it's nice to have a drink with my brother and sister like a normal person.

I've never really felt like a normal person if I'm honest. A normal person to me is someone who can keep their mental health in check. Who can get on with day to day life and still feel sane. I can't do that. I wake up and every second of my day is filled with ups and downs that I can't control. I can feel completely happy one second then ten minutes later I'm wondering why I'm bothering doing anything because we all die and nothing we do means anything in the end. I don't feel this way because of the drink. When I was a child I would cry in the middle of the night because I couldn't stop thinking about death and the fact I'm going to lose the ones I loved, I was terrified. I guess the drink was an escape. A way to take the edge of my constant overwhelming feelings and anxiety. To forget that we all die, and for a short while feel as if I can live forever.

The thought of being sober still scares me, but I want it now. I need it. I can't keep doing this over and over until I'm alone and have no one to pick me up when I fall. In a way I'm glad this has happened while I'm young. I have time on my side I suppose. Don't get me wrong I'm not one of these people who aren't realistic; I have a really long way to go, even if and when I get sober.

At least for the time being I can enjoy this night with my family, watch a good film and take a break from the hell that's become my everyday routine.

Today has been a good day.

Chapter 8: Faces on the wall

I got no sleep last night.

Don't get me wrong, I have tried my hardest. Pure terror and dread fills me every single time I put my head down. I'm scared to shut my eyes in case I start hearing things. When everyone goes to bed it's the hardest part of the day. I am alone in my room and feel like it's just me and my thoughts. So I drink, I keep drinking until I can't think anymore.

The cutting down hasn't been going well. I'm so terrified of having withdrawals I am drinking more than I need to. I am now drinking up to ten litres of cider a day. Obviously that's a lot, it sounds too much for a human to even ingest. Remember, I am being sick every half an hour and losing a lot of the alcohol that goes into my body.

I feel like shit. When I don't have a single bit of sleep my anxiety is worse than it already is and that's saying something. I at least tried to not drink for an hour, so my body could have some sort of break. Which obviously makes no sense but to me at the time it seemed like it would help.

The day trundles on like any other. Sitting in my room, drinking, watching YouTube videos, playing music (or attempting to) and playing on my games console.

My mum arrives home from work. I have asked her to pick me up my alcohol as I didn't want to leave the house today. We had a very heated over the phone as she didn't want to be picking me up drink, as it's killing me. I explain to her that not getting me the drink can equally kill me, so she reluctantly agrees.

She comes into my room.

"Okay, please don't call me and act like that when I'm at work, Jack. It's hard enough leaving you in the state you're in, I'm getting so upset at work."

"I know, I'm sorry, Mum, but I don't have anyone else here and I get worried"

She acknowledges this and puts down a bag in front of me.

"Now because you have been told to stick to what you need, and only what you need, I have got you these."

I look in the bag and it contains three small bottles of wine; the size of bottles you would get in a mini fridge at a hotel.

"Are you kidding… Please tell me you're kidding, Mum." I feel adrenaline pulse inside me. She can't be fucking serious. I need more than this.

"No, Jack, you don't need more than this, you have drunk all day and we have a bottle of cider still in the fridge. I don't want you having more than you need."

"I can't believe you. *Do you think this is a fucking game?*" I shout and I chuck the bag on the floor where the contents smash on the floor with a crunch.

My mum seems shocked but almost like she expected this, which breaks my heart a little.

"I'm not going to help you kill yourself, Jack. It is enough for tonight.

I start shouting. "Fucking hell, Mum! I don't need this right now! I need the fucking amount I need! *Are you fucking trying to kill me?*"

"I'm trying to keep you alive, Jacko!" She is crying now.

"This is a fucking joke. Fuck off then if you can't help me. Just fuck off."

She leaves the room in tears. I start to pick things up and smash objects around my room. All I can think of is drink. How did she think I would take this? I am fucked, I won't make it through the night with this much. I haven't slept and I need it to sleep. I'm going to withdraw. I just fucking know I will.

I can't calm down. I try to take my mind off it by playing on my console and this kills a couple of hours until my cider bottle is empty. The one from the fridge. Now I have nothing.

That bag. It has alcohol in it.

I move the bag and look inside. There is shattered glass swimming in a mix of alcohol. That is alcohol though. That can stop me from withdrawing.

I try my best to remove the biggest bits of glass that I can and I plunge my mouth into the mix.

I can feel small shards and spikes of glass in my mouth. I spit out what I can and continue lapping at it like a dog.

Is this what it has come to. What the fuck am I doing? I know this is madness but I don't care. I keep ingesting what I can.

I feel a sharp pain in my mouth. I've almost certainly just cut the roof of my mouth but I don't fucking care. I have to do this. To me this is necessary.

I spit onto the floor and I feel myself about to be sick.

"No, not now, not fucking now I need this," I say to myself.

Too late. I projectile vomit onto the floor and run to the toilet. Blood and vomit hit the porcelain. I cry hard.

I needed this inside me. And now it's not and I have to try and survive the night without any alcohol left.

I can't fucking bear this.

I stay in my room.

I can feel myself shaking violently. I feel numb, dizzy. I don't know why but I want to feel something.

I stand up and I walk around my room trying to get some feeling back in my body. Nothing. I say out loud: "It's fine, Jack, it's fine, you'll be okay, it's fine you'll be okay."

I still can't feel anything. I can't calm down.

I don't think. I head to the kitchen, grab a steak knife and swipe it on my arm. Blood immediately flows from the deep cut.

I can feel something now. It's warm and it covers my hand.

I head back to my room and sit. Blood pouring from my arm onto the floor. I look up and see a face forming on a blank wall of my room. It has extremely sharp features, devilish in appearance. It hovers on the wall with an appearance similar to the early stages of animation. Flickering and distorted.

It contorts and makes a grimace towards me. I stare and watch.

"This isn't real, Jack, this isn't fucking real," I tell myself.

The face moves around the wall, finding my eye line when I look away, taunting me. I can hear it speaking now, a faint fast talking. I can't make out what it is saying, the speaking is quick and low. I hear the word death. I cry out.

"Fuck off! Leave me alone! Leave me alone! *Leave me alone!*".

My mum bursts into the room.

"Oh my god, Jack, what have you done?"

She grabs my arm and runs to the kitchen. She wraps my hand in a kitchen towel and tells me to wait where I am.

I can still hear the face in the other room talking to me. I stare blankly into space. I feel numb now. I don't feel scared anymore. I feel like I don't care, to a degree that I don't care what happens to me now.

My mum enters with my coat and I notice she is wearing her Jacket over her pyjamas.

"Come on, we're going to the hospital," she says. She is crying again. Panicking.

She leads me towards the front door and we leave.

My mum leads me to the car door, opens it and sits me in the back seat.

My arms and legs are feeling very numb. I can feel a tingling sensation in my fingertips and my lips have gone numb.

"Mum I can't feel my legs…" I say, rubbing the parts of my body with no feeling frantically, trying to get some sensation back.

"I know, love, it's okay, we will be at the hospital in a minute just hold on."

My fingers and legs are jerking erratically. I don't have control anymore.

I feel a tight squeeze on my chest and my arms and legs lock up. My jaw is stiff, my fingers contort and I flop down onto the seats next to me, groaning.

My vision is strange, I can't stop daydreaming and I feel myself black in and out.

I scream out for help.

"Mum, I can't breathe…"

All the oxygen entering my mouth feels airless. There is no substance to it. I gasp for air frantically, it's still not enough. I pass out.

I wake again and I am shaking, not able to move.

"I don't want to die, Mum, I'm not ready…"

"You're not going to die, Jack!" she shouts through tears. I can feel we are going fast in the car.

"I'm sorry, Mum, I love you…"

"Jack, you're not going to die!! Try and calm your breathing! We're almost there!"

I black out again.

I come around just as we pull up to the hospital. I hear the unbuckling of a seat belt and a door slam. I don't hear my door open.

My mum appears a second later with a wheelchair and I am pulled upright. She moves me into the wheelchair, my legs still numb, trembling under my weight. My arms are locked up across my chest and my neck is fixed to the left, unable to move at all. I let out a groan. I feel so dizzy, so lightheaded and sick.

My mum rushes us to the front door and approaches the desk. There is a queue. I can make out that no one is coming over to help me.

"*Somebody fucking help me, please!*". I shout, without caring who is around me. I feel like I'm about to die. My mum apologises to the staff, I sit in the chair groaning. Tears roll down my cheek and I am unable to wipe them away.

I hear the footsteps of another person approaching. It's my gran. She rushes over to my mum looking horrified.

They speak to each other frantically in hushed tones, glancing at me as they speak.

I just don't want to die in front of my mum. It would break her.

My gran is a wonderful woman. A true patriarch of my family. She is loving, generous and courageous, I truly look up to her. An actress of the old school generation, she learned her craft in London, worked with some of the greats and saw the world.

She has very much been here for me in the same capacity as my mum. When my mum couldn't be here, my gran was, no questions asked. Even if my mum could be there, she would still be there too.

They are talking to the nurse at the desk. She is looking over at me sympathetically.

I feel myself getting tighter. My chest feels like someone is squeezing me of all my air.

The nurse comes over and starts wheeling me into another room. There are a number of beds all divided by blue curtains. It smells clinical in here.

There is a station in the middle of the room with doctors and nurses bustling to and from it. I am placed onto a hospital bed and realise I am being asked questions.

"How much have you drunk, Mr. Mackey? Can I call you Jack?"

"Yes."

"Okay, Jack, how much have you drunk tonight?"

"Around eight litres."

She is fitting a fabric contraption around my arm. She begins taking my blood pressure.

"And is that how much you usually drink?"

"No, I don't think so."

The nurse looks at the machine taking my blood pressure, slightly worried.

"Okay, so your blood pressure is quite high but that is to be expected if you are withdrawing."

She removes the strap from my bicep.

"Am I going to be okay?" I say. I'm crying now. I'm very scared. "I'm hallucinating again a lot," I say.

"I know, don't worry, Jack, we will get you something to help with that."

Just the same as before. Figures. One very large, dark, tall and menacing man stares at me from across the room. I can't make out a lot, he has very long black hair. His eyes are white, his face sunken and dead. Just staring at me.

I shut my eyes. This isn't real. I know this isn't real. It can't hurt me.

I feel someone hold my hand. My gran is sat by my bed, smiling.

"Oh, Jacko. What are we going to do, eh?" She smiles again.

"I know," I say. I'm trying to regulate my breathing. I feel like my body has had all of the energy removed from it. My chest feels incredibly hot. A constant sickness sits on my ribcage.

I'm going to be sick.

I throw my head over the edge of my bed. I vomit onto the floor. Red and yellow. A lot of blood and old cider sat in my stomach. It fucking hurts.

My chest feels as if someone has taken a serrated knife and plunged it down my throat.

"Oh god…" I say, trying desperately to catch my breath.

My gran hands me a cardboard container to be sick in.

"I'm sorry." I say, head in my hands, trembling.

"You don't need to apologise, darling."

I feel her hand on my arm and I feel comforted.

"Where's mum?" I say.

"She's talking to the nurses. Explaining the situation."

I try to listen for her but I can't hear her. No mother should have to see her son this way. The guilt is overwhelming. The sadness in my heart is crippling me of rational thought.

I am violently sick into the container.

"Fuuuuuck…" I say, crying.

"I know, Jacko, I know," my gran says, holding my arm, comforting me.

A doctor enters.

"Hello, Jack. Not feeling too well I see."

"No, not well," I say, head still in my hands.

"Okay, well a nurse will be in with you in a moment to give you some fluids and vitamins," he says looking at my gran.

"Can I have something to stop my anxiety? I feel like I'm going to die."

"Well, yes, we may give you something for that, for now just the fluids."

He walks out.

I feel as though I am a burden. I guess they know I've been here before. They know addicts relapse and there isn't much they can do about that.

I keep my eyes shut. Every time they open I'm seeing something disturbing. The tall dark man is still staring at me across the room. He won't leave. I know it's not real. Yet if I know it's not real, then why the fuck is it still there? It's my brain doing this so surely me knowing it's a hallucination tells my brain that.

I don't know anymore.

I just know that it's fucking terrifying regardless.

I hear what sounds like African tribe chanting coming from somewhere. I open one eye and look in the direction of the wall where the noise is coming from. There is a line of African tribesman on the wall, walking in a never ending circle to their chanting.

I mean where the fuck has this come from. If my brain is creating this stuff I have no idea where it got this from.

They are in the form of a cartoon drawing. In the same style cartoon as the 'Popeye the sailor man' cartoon I used to watch when I was younger.

Over and over and over. This chanting plays on a loop in my head.

I hold my hands up to my ears and shut my eyes. As soon as I do the sound switches from hearing it aloud, to hearing it in my head. I can't escape it. It's never ending.

A nurse enters.

She hooks up my arm to a cannula and attaches the cannula to a bag of yellow liquid.

"Is that the vitamins? Will that stop my withdrawals?" I say desperately.

"This will help your body get the nutrients it needs. You're losing a lot of essential liquids and vitamins so this helps."

"Is it Pabrinex?" I say.

She looks at me and smiles. "The fact you know what it is says that you need it."

"I know, unfortunately I've been in this position before."

"Well, let's make this the last time, eh?" she replies, smiling.

She exits and my mum enters.

She smiles at my gran. She looks like she's been crying.

"Okay, Mum?" she says to my gran.

"Yes, darling, were you talking to the doctor?"

"Yeah, they don't have enough beds tonight and I've asked to speak to the person in charge of the ward. I said to them if Jack goes home I'm scared for him, it seems they just need the beds for other people."

This news hurts to hear. I could die and they want to give my bed to someone else. I can't go home. I will keep hallucinating.

"Fucking hell, I'm going to die, aren't I."

"Jacko, you are *not going to die!!*" says my gran firmly. She looks worried but I believe her when she says this.

"There's a lot of other people very ill, sweetheart. These other people aren't ill through alcohol either so they have to prioritize," my mum says.

I know this is right. Other people didn't ask for their illnesses. I guess I have myself to blame for this, I shouldn't have ever taken another drink. I am still angry though.

"They need to have a separate section for people sick like me don't they," I say.

"If only the NHS had that type of money, love!" my mum says.

I know what amazing work the people at this hospital do. They saved my life once before. I can't expect them to jump and do it again just because I am withdrawing again. I still feel angry though. There is so much prejudice against addicts.

There is always an air of 'look what you have done again' from the doctors, which makes me incredibly angry. Sometimes you luck out and get a doctor who really knows a lot about addiction, but most the time, there is prejudice.

The fact is my mental health needs sorting. I can't get my mental health fixed while I'm drinking, so it's a vicious circle. I can't live with my thoughts and feelings so I drink, but the drink stops me getting mental help.

The sad fact is (and I can only speak for myself) but I feel that there are a lot of alcoholics out there that have mental health problems and can't get it treated because they are using, even though they are using to cope.

"Can I have some water?"

My mum looks in her bag and hands me a bottle of water.

I drink. I can't remember the last time I drank water. Genuinely. I never drink it. The only thing I drink every single day is cider so it feels odd.

"Thank you."

"That's okay, love."

I shut my eyes again and try to rest. Which feels impossible the way I'm feeling but I try anyway.

Before I get the chance to, someone enters with a cart.

"Okay, Jack, sorry, I need to get a look at your arm."

It's the nurse from before. Jesus, I forgot about my arm. The last thing on my mind if I'm honest. It doesn't hurt, but I know it's very deep, so I agree to have her take a look.

She removes the kitchen towel and I feel the dried blood tear on the fabric. Then I feel warmth cover my arm, fresh blood falling to my hand.

"Oh wow, you've really done a number on yourself!" she says.

I can't see what she is doing. I am not squeamish, I just don't really care about the cut.

"Okay, that's definitely going to need stitches. I can see your white tissue of your arm, you were very close to the bone."

"Really? I didn't even realise if I'm honest," I say, still not looking.

My mum and gran can see it and are making painful faces. I guess the fact I feel numb all over has helped on this occasion. The nurse begins to clean the wound. It's now I feel the pain. Hot, stinging pain. A very dull ache surrounds the cut.

"Okay, Jack, I am going to start stitching it back up, I've numbed the area but let me know if you feel anything and I can numb it some more."

"Okay."

She begins stitching up my arm. I can't feel anything, just tugging and the feeling of thread looping in and out.

"You feel okay?" she says.

"Yeah, I'm fine," I say.

She continues, telling me I'm doing great etcetera. She finishes and tells me it's all done. I say thank you and look at my arm. The cut has shrunk and I can barely see it. Dried blood stains my arm.

"Thank you very much," I say as she stands up to leave.

"You're very welcome, Jack, I hope you feel better soon." She smiles and leaves.

My mum stands up again and follows the nurse out of the room.

"Where is she going?" I ask my gran.

"I'm not sure."

She is gone for around five minutes and returns looking slightly positive.

"I just spoke to the doctor and they are moving you in a minute."

"Oh, where to?" I say.

"I'm not sure but we will be speaking to the head of the ward when you're moved," she says.

I nod. I don't really know what I'm going to say to this person.

"Why are we seeing the head person?"

"We need to explain the situation to her, love, and explain how bad you are at the moment."

"Right, okay, but surely they can just look at me. I look like shit?" I say, semi jokingly.

"Evidently not. It's either that or we have to go home again," says my mum to my gran.

"Oh my god. I can't go home," I say, anxiety filling me up.

"Well that's why we are going to speak to this person!"

"Okay…"

Chapter 9: Night Time visitor

A large gentleman approaches my bed and tells me we are being moved to another ward. I gather my things and stand up with the help of my mum. We follow him into a narrow corridor, where he tells me to take a seat on some chairs outside an office. Me, my mum and my gran sit.

The large, very dark man has followed me. He is standing at the end of the corridor, staring with white, dead eyes directly at me.

I shut mine tight. I focus on my breathing and try my best not to think about it.

"*You, boy!*" I hear the man shout from the end of the corridor. His shout is muffled, like he is shouting from beneath a pillow, but the voice is harsh and gravelly, sending chills up my spine and making me leap to my feet.

"Fuck this," I say.

"What, love? What's the matter?" My mum and gran have got to their feet also and are looking at me concerned.

"There's a huge man near the end of the corridor over there, he's shouting at me."

"Jack, no one is there, remember it's not real, it can't hurt you. Sit down with us, it won't hurt you love." My mum gives me a hug and sits me down on the plastic chair.

"I know but it doesn't make it any less real for me. I can see it and hear it. I know it's not real but this is horrific," I say. Resting my face in my hands, I feel exhausted.

"I know, love, but just remember it's your brain doing this," she says.

"I know, I know."

We wait for around an hour before we are finally seen.

A tall woman called Jane, in her late forties, exits the office and asks me and my mum inside. My gran waits outside.

We sit in two chairs facing her desk and she sits down and addresses us.

"So the nurses mentioned you wanted to speak to me, Mrs. Mackey? How can I help?"

"Yes, basically, Jack was in with you a while ago for an alcohol detox due to acute withdrawal. He was experiencing severe hallucinations and it was extremely serious. He unfortunately didn't have any after care when he left hospital and we weren't sure on what the protocol was. Jack unfortunately relapsed and since has been getting just as bad as before. He has been hallucinating, self-harming, not eating and not sleeping. Your nurses mentioned they may send Jack home today and I wanted to see you to ask if you can please help us. Jack wants sobriety. He has no life at the moment and neither do I. I don't want to watch my son kill himself anymore and we are both completely exhausted and at the end of our rope…"

My mum is upset. Very upset. She is noticeably frustrated and saddened at the thought that I could be sent home when I'm still extremely ill.

"I see," says the doctor. "Well, the problem is, we currently have no free beds for Jack tonight. And due to the fact there are countless admissions with life threatening cases in ECT, we can't give Jack a bed over these people. If we had the beds it would be very different but the fact is we just don't."

My mum exhales, tears running down her cheek. "Please. Please. Is there anything you can do."

"Can I say something?" I speak up.

"Yes, of course," Jane replies.

"I know I relapsed. I know it looks like I don't want to be sober. But I do. I didn't relapse because I like being this way. I struggle with my mental health and drinking is my way of self-medicating that. I see now that alcohol makes things worse, but it's just a fact that it's what I did to cope. If I go home tonight, I am genuinely worried I will kill myself. I cannot live like this. I know you hear about these symptoms but living them is a whole different story. I can't sit at home with figures threatening me and saying they want to kill me and not want to take my own life. Death would be easier, more peaceful. I can't put my mum through this anymore and I can't guarantee my safety at home. I'm incredibly scared and I am begging for your help."

"Can you not just keep him in for one night? To get him past this night and get him slightly back on his feet. He hasn't slept in days." My mum is sobbing, as am I.

Jane goes quiet. She looks at me seriously and at my mum sympathetically.

"Okay. The only thing I can do is keep him in overnight in our EAU unit. This won't be a detox. It will keep you stable for the night so you can get some vitamins inside you and we can stabilise your withdrawal for the night. Now, this isn't us being able to cure you, Jack. When you leave you will still be dependant but tonight we will keep you in, just to make sure you don't hurt yourself and to give your poor mum a break because she looks exhausted."

I smile. My mum smiles.

"That's all I'm asking for, I just need to sleep and stop hallucinating," I say.

"Okay. Well we will transfer you into their care in a moment, and we will also call crisis team due to the fact you feel suicidal and are scared for your own life."

"Okay, yeah, that sounds good," says my mum.

"Thank you so much, you have no idea what this means to me," I say, as we stand and I shake her hand.

"That no problem, Jack, let's get you sorted and leave your mum to get some sleep."

My mum smiles and thanks her.

I am taken into the EAU (emergency assessment unit) and I am given a hospital bed. This ward of the hospital contains other people kept in for the night. One is another alcoholic. I can hear him shouting, nonstop. He is shouting for help, over and over. Someone goes to him and asks him to keep his noise down, and that a nurse will be with him soon. He is alone and scared, this upsets me a lot.

I lay down. I am still shaking and sweating. The hallucinations are still here, but I am learning to not let them frighten me as much. I am somewhere that is safe, that is all that matters.

My mum and gran sit next to me and a male nurse comes to my side. He explains he will be giving me small doses of Librium and Pabrinex. The Librium is for withdrawals and the Pabrinex for my vitamins. He also gives me a sleeping tablet (Most likely diazepam) and leaves me to sleep.

My mum explains that she is going to head home, but my gran agrees to stay and look over me until morning. I hug my mum goodbye and tell her I'm sorry. Not just for this but for the previous night and how I acted. She tells me to just get some sleep and that she loves me. I say it back and watch her go.

My gran and I sit and talk for a while. I begin to get sleepy and my gran has begun to fall asleep in the chair next to my bed. Out of the corner of my eye, I see a silvery outline. It is pitch black in the ward, and most people are asleep.

The outline is around five foot tall. I look closer and it looks to be an elderly woman. Her eyes are bright silver, I can see through her body and she is moving very, very slowly. The figure looks lost, completely alone and scared. I try to avoid its gaze, but it seems I have drawn its attention.

It approaches me very, very slowly. Not saying a word although its mouth is moving very fast, like its muttering something under its breath.

It's next to my bed. Inching closer and closer to my face.

I turn my head and try to ignore it but it seems impossible. I turn my head back and it is inches from my face. I can feel the cold breath exhaling its mouth, as it mutters frantically under its breath:

"I don't know where I am, I don't know who I am, I don't know where I'm going. I don't know where I am, I don't know who I am, I don't know where I'm going. I don't know where I am, I don't know who I am, I don't know where I'm going."

Again, the voice sounds as though the volume has been turned down. As if it is speaking under its breath to me but it can't speak louder than a mouse. I stay where I am.

I look through the face inches away from mine and stay completely still. I say nothing, I don't acknowledge it. I just stare through its misty body to the wall ahead.

As slowly as it approached, it backs away. Turning its head, it moves towards another patient's cubicle. I see it pass through the curtains. And it's gone.

I exhale, look up at the ceiling and wish for sleep. I shut my eyes.

Finally.

Chapter 10: Fast-tracked

I wake up and I'm drenched in sweat. My gran is asleep next to me on an uncomfortable looking chair. I look around expecting to see hallucinations and I see none. I'm still shaking and I feel like I've been hit by a truck, but I am alive.

I lay in silence for a minute. I say silence, the man two cubicles across from me is still shouting, has been most of the night. I think it's not just alcohol he is in for. It sounds as though he attempted suicide from what I overheard. I wonder how my mum is, whether she got any sleep. I hope she did. I feel the familiar swell of guilt in my stomach. I ride it out and sit with it. I need to feel this sober. I deserve this feeling. I put so much on my family and I don't deserve not to feel this.

My gran stirs and wakes. She looks exhausted.

"Morning, Gran."

"Morning, sweetheart, how did you sleep? Did you get any sleep?"

"I did funnily enough, didn't think I would. I'm soaked though."

"Oh dear. Well at least you got some sleep at last."

There is a nurses' station at the entrance to the ward and I see them talking to each other and going through charts. I don't know how they do it. I don't think I would ever be smart enough to do what they do. A small male nurse approaches my bed.

"Mr. Mackey, how did we sleep?"

"Good I think, I'm soaked through with sweat, is that normal?"

"That's your body getting rid of all the toxins basically. The whole ward heard you snoring so you definitely did sleep."

He laughs and passes me some pills in a paper cup.

"This is Librium and some vitamins for you."

I empty the contents into my mouth and swallow.

"Thank you so much."

"You're welcome," he responds smiling. "Your mum called this morning to check how you were."

I smile. "Oh right, yeah… she is good like that," I say.

"Yeah, she sounds like a lovely lady!" he says, picking up my chart and scanning it.

"She is!" my gran says, beaming.

"So, a member of the crisis team is on their way. She is a lovely woman and is looking forward to speaking with you." He puts down my chart.

"That's great, thank you so much, you guys really don't know how much it meant to me, letting me stay," I say, feeling myself getting choked up.

"That's what we are here for!" he says, smiling. "I will be back in a while to check on you, Jack, see you in a while."

"Thank you so much," says my gran.

"So that's good, Jack, she is on her way and maybe we can get some help from her?" Gran looks at me positively and smiles.

"Yeah, I hope so, they haven't been great before. Then again I've never been this bad before," I respond.

"True, true," she says, looking down at her phone.

"I'll give your mum a call and let her know what's happening."

"Okay, sounds good," I say.

I think about the last time I was here. If I had known how fast I would relapse, would I have started drinking again. I suppose because I didn't have the after care or know the dangers, I thought I could go back to my old ways. The truth is when this is over, when I have been into detox and I have wiped my life clean of this, I don't think I'll miss it.

I miss eating. I miss sleeping. I miss waking up and wondering what to do with my day, I miss it when my world was full of possibilities. I miss my days not being controlled by a bottle. I miss my family and what used to be. This isn't me anymore, this is a disgusting mask I can't take off. Fused to an ugly face I don't recognise anymore.

I wish I could have been someone who could just have one. I've never been able to do that in any aspect of my life. It's always been all or nothing. It's just how I'm wired.

I watch a patient opposite to me. She is old, around late eighties. She looks like she is struggling to breathe. She is alone. I wish people never had to be alone. No one deserves that. There is nothing I'm more scared of than that.

I like to people watch. It helps me understand my own mortality sometimes. I like to put myself in their shoes, even for just ten minutes. An escape from my life and picturing what it must be like to live from a completely different perspective. I think the Librium is kicking in. I'm feeling very light and calm. If they sold this in shops I would definitely have this instead. Again. This is my nature.

"Mum's coming on her break, Jacko." My gran returns with a coffee and a bottle of orange juice for me. "Got you this, darling." She passes me the bottle.

"Thank you, Gran that's lovely." I open the bottle and drain it. I must've been thirsty. I feel as if I'm hungry. I'm scared to eat. Every time I eat my withdrawal gets worse.

"Do you reckon they do food in here?" I ask.

"I saw someone at the end there eating earlier," she responds. "I can check to see if you can have anything if you would like?"

"Yes please," I say, my mouth is watering. I feel sick. Is this hunger or sickness? I can't tell the difference anymore.

My gran goes to check about food and I take out my phone. No missed calls or texts.

I haven't told anyone what is going on. Isaac knew that I was drinking again but I can't tell him every time I have a funny turn. I flick through my social media then set my phone down. I never feel better after looking at it. It's just people posting pictures of amazing things I can never do.

I set my phone down and exhale. I'm shaking but not quite as much. The pills are doing their job.

My gran returns with a plate of toast.

"They grabbed this from the breakfast service for you."

She places the plate down in front of me. I am really nervous about this. It's intimidating, and I start to regret asking for it.

I know I have to eat it. I have to eat something. I haven't eaten in a long time. I butter the toast and slice it into quarters. I take a breath and I eat.

It sounds ridiculous but it tastes like the best thing I've ever eaten. I have to remind myself to slow down if I eat too quickly I'll be sick. I eat slowly. Taking in the moment. Again this is something which helps me feel like a normal human being.

I finish two quarters of the toast and I stop. I can feel the food in my stomach. I keep it there. I am determined. I will not let this beat me anymore. I have to eat. Even if it makes me feel worse. I will die if I don't.

"Well done, Jacko," my gran says, grinning with glee at the fact I managed some food.

"I don't think I can have anymore," I say.

"And you don't have to, but you have eaten *something*, that's what matters."

I love her for this. She didn't put any pressure on me to eat. She knows what a big deal this is for me and I feel good that I ate. It's the small things.

An hour or so passes and the woman from the mental health team arrives. She is very small and walks over to my bed at a brisk pace.

"Hello, Jack! My name is Alice and I am from the mental health team put forward for you. How are you feeling?"

She has a very strong Nigerian accent and is wearing large glasses that cover most of her face.

"I've been better, nice to meet you, this is my gran, Jennie."

Alice walks over to my gran, introduces herself and sits on another chair next to my bed.

"You had a very rough night, I hear?"

"Yeah, you could say that. I'm feeling slightly better today but still feel dreadful," I say.

"Of course, yes, I can imagine," she says.

I notice her eyes drop to my arm.

"This is not good is it?" she says playfully.

"No, not good," I respond. I smile, embarrassed.

"Well, Jack, I know a little about your case and frankly I'm very concerned about you. I am very confused as to why you are not getting the help you need?"

She is looking at me seriously. I feel already comfortable with her.

"Well, I have been told I am on the list for detox but I am still waiting for the date I'm going in."

She nods listening. "Okay, well what alcohol addiction service are you with?"

"CRI in Tunbridge wells," I say.

"Okay, well I have some notes here from last night and I have been informed about your situation with the alcohol. I will call them and put forward my recommendation that you are put in there sooner rather than later."

Alice is showing me her notes as she talks.

"Did they give these to you?" I say.

"No, I was on the phone with them early this morning and I also met with the doctor who was treating you. I also have information about when you were last in hospital," she says showing me the particular notes.

"Wow," I say grinning.

"What?" she says smiling back at me.

"It's really nice to see you actually know about what I'm going through. Whatever you can do would go a long way. I only feel suicidal because the alcohol is controlling my life. I drink because I have to now. I don't feel like I am living. It's just existing." I am shocked at how well I can speak today. I feel anxious but as I said I feel comfortable with Alice.

"Yes of course," Alice says referencing her notes again. "Well, I will call CRI and we will get this moving as you can't live like this. I spoke to your mum on the phone and she is so worried about you."

I didn't realise she had spoken to my mum. I guess that's how she knows about a lot more than appears on paper.

"I know, she is amazing, I wouldn't be here without her, or my gran."

Alice looks at my gran and nods, smiling and watching me patiently.

"Let me get on the phone with them and see what I can find out," she says.

"Okay, that sounds amazing."

She nods, shakes my hand and tells me she will be back in a while.

I turn to my gran.

"I did not expect that."

"Neither did I! Have you seen these people before," Gran replies looking taken aback.

"Yes, but they sent someone else who just kind of noted how I was and then checked in with me at home, nothing this in depth," I say.

"Well let's hope something comes of this," she says.

"I know, let's hope."

We sit and talk for a while. My mum arrives looking concerned but rested.

"Hey, Jacko."

"Hey mum, you okay?"

"I'm fine, sweetheart, how are you? Did you manage to get any sleep? I spoke to Alice on the phone, she seems really on the ball, thank god!"

"I know, she is great. Yeah, I managed to get some sleep, and I ate something, thank god. Only a bit of toast but it's something."

"That's great, love, really great."

My mum sits down next to my gran and gives her a hug. My gran updates her on what is going on and I decide I want a cigarette. I haven't had one for a while and really could use one.

"I'm going to try and go for a cigarette," I say.

My mum looks worried. "I don't know if you can love…"

"Course I can, I did when I was here before?"

She nods, remembering, and I walk out of the unit and into the fresh air.

The light is blinding. It's very cold and there is a streak of sunlight draped across the entrance of A & E. I pull out my tobacco, roll a cigarette and light it up. I'm still shaking slightly. Maybe that's the cold. I take a long drag of the cigarette.

I sit against the cold wall on the floor to the right of the doors and smoke. My head feels light and clouded. Head rush. A free high. I sit with it and shut my eyes.

People stare at me as they walk in and out. I don't care. I know what I am and what I look like. I can't change that, but I can enjoy this cigarette.

I watch a family walk into the hospital and I feel sad.

I feel I will never have that. Never have children and never be happy. The way things are, I don't know how I would ever get to a place where that is possible for me.

I wish I was healthy like them, I wish I wasn't this.

I stand up and stamp out my cigarette.

I walk inside, towards my bed and climb in. Alice has returned and is sitting speaking to my mum. They are deep in conversation and don't acknowledge me as I return.

"Everything okay?" I say to my mum.

"Sorry, love. Yes, Alice just got off the phone with Tracey at CRI."

"Oh really? What did she say?" I say, I am interested to see where this goes, I don't have high hopes.

"I have informed Tracey of how bad things have got, the self-harm and the delirium. And she is speaking to the higher ups today. It looks as though you may be off to detox by the end of the week." Alice smiles at me and my mum and gran look relieved.

"Really?" I say, shocked.

"Yes, Jack. Obviously, we still have to wait to hear what they say, but Tracey feels positive that this will be the outcome."

I can't believe it. It feels like a trick. I am excited. I am scared. I don't know what to think.

"This isn't going to not materialise, though, is it? I can't deal with waiting longer than that, I am scared for my life and I don't know what I will do…" I'm not entirely sure why but I am crying now.

"This is what I have explained to her and she seems very confident. She is rushing to get this sorted out for you. She is a wonderful lady!"

"So are you!" I say, smiling through tears at Alice.

"Oh, you're very kind, Jack, I just want to see you get better, that is all." She is smiling and I notice my mum is crying, she seems happy but is crying. "There is a lot more we need to go through to do with keeping in touch and getting you the right medication you need. Shall we get started on this now?" She looks at my mum and they nod at each other. "Okay, wonderful, sorry, Jack, this is the boring bit," Alice says.

I don't mind. I don't mind at all. It feels like this still may not happen. I have been told many times in the past that I will get help and it has never happened. I have been to this exact hospital, many times before, withdrawing and been turned away with nothing but diazepam in my pocket, defeated and devastated.

I guess I never had the help of Tracey before. Or Alice for that matter. This feels different, it feels official and they seem sure. All I can do is hold out until that day comes.

The male nurse returns to my bed and picks up my chart.

"Excuse me, sorry. When I go back home what is the plan? Do I have to keep drinking?" I say to the nurse.

"Let me get hold of the doctor for you, Jack, and we will go through it."

"Okay thank you," I say.

"You will have to keep drinking, Jacko, that's what the doctor said last night," my mum says.

I remember and feel a weight being lifted back onto my chest.

I don't know why I forgot. I guess I felt normal for a while.

A doctor walks over with the male nurse. He is clearly very rushed off his feet, he looks stressed. He has a yellow and black tie on with three pens neatly tucked in his shirt pocket.

"So, Mr. Mackey. You have been with us overnight, receiving Librium and Pabrinex, how are you feeling?"

He isn't looking at me. He is staring at the clip board in front of him.

"Er, yeah not great, still pretty shaken."

"Yes well, obviously this isn't a permanent solution, you will have to continue to consume what you were before to keep yourself out of withdrawal, but you knew that, didn't you? Have you discussed your after care with Alice?" he looks to Alice and she nods her head.

"Yeah, CRI are going to try to get me into detox this week," I say.

"Okay, that's good. Well if you have any questions, you are okay to leave."

"Okay, thank you for keeping me over night," I respond.

"No problem, take care of yourself and I hope detox goes well." He smiles at me and my mum and leaves.

"I guess that's that then..." I say, a bit shocked at the speed at which I was just seen.

"I guess he is very busy," my mum says to Alice.

"Looks like it!" Alice says. She is packing up her papers and hands my mum some paperwork.

"Alice, thank you. For everything," I say. I really mean it. Not many people show sympathy and compassion for addicts and this was a really lovely change.

"You're more than welcome, Jack, and I really hope the detox goes well. Just make sure you try to keep yourself positive before you get there. Also I know you don't want to, but you need to drink the same amount you were before you withdrew to keep the withdrawals at bay."

"Yeah, got it, thank you."

Alice gets up and gives my mum and gran a hug. She smiles, waves and walks away.

"Okay, Jacko, you ready?" my mum says.

"Yeah, I think so."

I get myself off the bed and pull on my Jacket. I say goodbye to the nurses who helped me and head towards the exit.

I say a big thank you to my gran and give her a hug. She says she will follow me and my mum back in her car and come for a cup of tea. Me and my mum get in the car and I put on my seat belt. My mum leans over and gives me a long, tight hug.

"I love you, Jacko, I'm sorry I wasn't there overnight."

"Mum, don't be silly, I am sorry about everything, literally it's been a nightmare, I am sorry."

"The important thing is you're getting the help you need, that's all that matters love."

Mum smiles at me and starts the car. I remind her before we set off we need to pick up alcohol. Timing isn't great, always bloody asking her for stuff. She acknowledges and we drive out of the car park.

I feel nervous about going back. One more week. That's all, one more week.

Chapter 11: Losing control

Haven't slept and been up for a while now. Had a call from Tracey. My date for detox is set for next week. That was yesterday. I left hospital last week and when I returned home there was a lot of waiting. Waiting to hear the news.

I let out a cry of relief when I was told about Bright House. That's the name of the detox facility. I have seen some pictures. From what I can tell it's an old oast house that has been renovated into an alcohol detox centre.

I'm so nervous. I know it sounds ridiculous. I'm really scared. I am scared I will pass away and my family won't be there so I can say goodbye, and that I am sorry.

I feel so fucking sad all the time right now. I can't stop thinking about the bad things I have done. The people I have hurt. The mess I've made. And what will be the mark I've made on this earth? Nothing, as of yet.

I am told to bring the following:
- Pyjamas
- Slippers
- Books
- Necessary medication

Mobile phones are not allowed in the detox facility. There is a phone available after two days of your stay, for you to call family members and friends. Before you arrive, drink only enough to stop withdrawals, no more.

Smoking is allowed at the facility, in the garden. Strictly no smoking in rooms.

Rooms are strictly one per person.

I read the rules and what to bring, then unfold a map of how to get there.

I don't understand why they have given us this. We have sat nav so it'll be fine.

I decide to go for a walk.

I wouldn't usually, but I'm going mad sitting in my room. There is only so much staring at my TV I can do. I leave my front door, turn right and head towards a field next to my house. As I walk along the path I can see someone in the allotment near the field, digging, red faced and tired. Their radio cries out tinny classical music. I hold my hand up to wave. They wave back.

I put my headphones on and listen to some music. I like acoustic indie music at the moment. I reach a bench at the far end of the field and I sit and listen.

I have a flask in my inside pocket with cider in it. I open it and drink some.

I sit and watch dog walkers, runners and families pass by.

I think the best way for me to not worry about detox is just to not think about it. It's the safest place for me to go and I will be sober by the end. That's all that matters. I have said to some of my friends I will try to go up to London and watch Isaac's band play in Hyde Park. I figure that it's near the end of the week and I can make sure I don't withdraw whilst I'm there. I want to support his band. Both he and Laurie the guitarist have been great friends and I haven't been around, which I feel sad about.

My stomach churns. The thought of being around so many people is terrifying but something I want to do before I get sober.

My stomach isn't feeling great actually. Why the fuck did I walk so far from my house.

Since all I ingest is acidic cider and basically a slice of toast a day, it's safe to say my insides are fucked.

I get up and I walk towards the doctor's surgery situated on a path just off the field. Closer to me then my house.

I'm sweating. Jesus, I feel awful.

This really isn't good. I've not been caught short before and I don't really want to start today if I'm honest.

A small elderly lady is in front of me. I walk fast around her like some odd speed walker and head towards the surgery.

I am focusing on the floor and breathing slowly. My anxiety is making this a million times worse. Why didn't I take some fucking Imodium? Jesus Christ.

I keep focused on the pavement and reach the gate: CLOSED

Fuck! I look at my phone and didn't even notice the time. The place is fucking shut.

What.... am I going to do.

I start jogging towards my house. Immediately I realise that is a bad idea. Funnily enough when you have an awful stomach jogging isn't the best idea.

This can't happen. Seriously this cannot happen. I can't breathe. I'm panicking and I can't believe this... *fuck... no.*

There isn't anything I can do. It's happened. The old lady I passed is now near to where I stand. She notices my visible anguish and approaches me.

"Is everything okay? You look very pale?"

"Yeah, fine, sorry, fine, " I say rudely. I can't help it, being short with her.

The last thing I need is to be in a conversation. I need to get fucking home. I can't believe this is my life now. I can't even go for a walk without something bad happening.

Uncomfortable is an understatement. I can't think about what has happened I have to focus on getting home, I am not well at all.

I walk through the allotments and onto the path back to my house. I can feel myself about to cry but I don't. I stop myself and focus on my house.

I'm walking up my drive, I open the front door and I run upstairs.

I look at myself in the mirror, pale, skinny and bloated. I cry hard. I brace myself for what's to come.

This tops the list of worst things that has ever happened to me.

I climb into the bath and I run the water. I take off my jeans.

I have no words.

I clean myself best I can. There is blood, not a lot, but there is shit and blood.

I cry. I climb out of the bath and I put bleach into the bath and I rinse it. I get the boiling hot water and I run it into the bath.

I clean up.

I throw up.

I add more bleach.

I scrub.

I finish and I get into the shower. I wash myself clean and I let the water fall on my face while I cry. I touch my stomach and it is tender and sore. I wash my hair, which I haven't done in a while. I lean against the wall and try to compute what just happened.

I feel ashamed. I feel sick and disgusting. I feel how I look.

I exit the shower when I am sure I am clean and I dry myself. My chest is shallow but my stomach is ballooned out. The cider bloats me and it hurts.

My arms are thin and my face is gaunt and anaemic.

I'm so tired. Just a few more days. This will be a bad memory and I can start again. Just a few more days.

I walk downstairs to my room. Pull on some jogging bottoms and a shirt and open my cider. I drink three pints fast. I push my sadness down. I let the drink take over. I let it comfort me in ways no one else can.

I sit and put on some music. I listen. I shut my eyes.

Tears keep coming, streaming down my cheeks and I stay silent. I don't want what just happened to be real and send me down a dark path today.

I keep my eyes shut and I listen to the music.

I try to forget.

I wake up and it's dark.

I get up, drink a glass of cider and head upstairs.

The jeans I was wearing are still in the bath with the bleach; I forgot about them.

I take them out and they are ruined. I go back downstairs and throw them in the bin outside. I feel weak and sick. I go back inside and I pour myself another glass of cider. I breathe in, exhale and down the drink.

I hear my mum in the kitchen. She comes into my room.

"Hey, Jacko, you okay? You were asleep when I got in."

"I've had the day from hell."

"I know, love, not long until this is a bad memory though."

"No not just a normal horrible day. I shit myself while I was walking in the park."

Hearing myself say it I start to grin. I don't know why, it sounds hilarious when I say it out loud. My mum sees my grin and returns it.

"Noooo!" she says, trying to hide her grin behind her hands.

"Yup. I feel disgusting, I can't believe it happened." I feel sad and shameful about it but for some reason I can't stop smiling and I start laughing.

"Oh my god, what did you do?" my mum says, also laughing now.

"What could I do? I had to get back here as fast as I could! An old lady tried to talk to me when it happened, I just walked off, and it was awful."

She is really laughing now.

"I don't know why *you're* laughing, Mum."

She looks at me. "You're laughing too? Why shouldn't I? You have to laugh about these things! Why shouldn't I laugh about it?" she says.

"They were your jeans I was wearing, you lent them to me last week…" I say, now laughing hard.

Her face drops. "You're kidding me. Jacko! For god's sake!" She looks pissed off but is still smiling and laughing. "What did you do with them?!"

"I had to put them in the bin, they were ruined," I say.

"Well, I suppose you couldn't help it, could you. I'm kind of glad you didn't try and wash them and then give them back, I don't think I would want them."

"Yeah, I did think that."

It feels good to laugh. Especially about something as horrible as this. My mum is right. It's all you can do in these situations. I feel better already about it.

"Do you feel okay now?" my mum says.

"I do feel a bit better now. There was blood and everything, it was awful."

"Oh Jesus, love. Well, I'm sure that's because of all the acid in your stomach. It will be okay, tell them all of this when you get to detox. Okay?"

"You're fucking kidding, aren't you? I'm not telling them I shit myself!"

My mum laughs again. "I don't mean tell everyone, just the doctors," she says.

"Oh, okay, yeah I will."

My mum hugs me and heads out of my room.

I follow her into the kitchen.

"Mum, I've been invited to watch Isaac in Hyde Park at the end of the week."

"I don't think that's a good idea Jack…" my mum says.

"I know. It's not like I will be relapsing though, I'm already drinking and if I make sure I take Imodium and stuff before I should be okay. I really want to see everyone before I go into detox."

"Well, see how you feel about it tomorrow. There is no use making yourself worse before detox," she says.

"Yeah, okay, I'll wait. Thanks, Mum."

"No problem, sweetheart."

I hug her again and head to bed. Tomorrow's a new day, can't be as bad as today. Surely.

Chapter 12: Music vitality

I have decided to go to London. I am really nervous about it but if I make sure I have Imodium and the correct amount of alcohol I should be fine. I need to see my friends. I haven't had contact with anyone really since the gig when I relapsed.

When I went to see my sister I managed to keep myself withdrawal free most of the day.

So this should be manageable.

I tell my mum my plan and she looks worried.

"Okay, well if you feel the slightest bit like you are feeling off, come home."

"I will," I promise her.

I have a couple of days until I leave for detox. I want one last time, to see my friends as a drinker. I know that sounds stupid. After this I will be sober, and the dynamic will change a lot. I am worried about this. I know my friends will accept this but I am also scared of being seen as boring. I suppose I would rather be boring than dead.

I head to the shop down my road and I pick up a pack of Imodium, some cigarettes and some cider I haven't had before. I don't know why today of all days

I've changed. This cider is stronger, around 8.5 percent alcohol and I can assume it's going to taste like shit.

At this point all cider tastes like shit to me so I don't care. The higher the percentage, the less likely I am to go into withdrawal.

I head back to my house, sit down and open a can of the new stuff. I down a pint of it. Fuck. It tastes what I can imagine paint stripper tastes like. I don't care, I can add some fruit juice to it or something.

I go upstairs and get in the shower, shave and get ready. I look in the mirror.

There really is nothing I can do about how terrible I look. There are blotches on my face from blood vessels that have popped whilst I've been sick. My neck is very thin, my cheeks are sunken and grey.

I try to make an effort. I wear a leather Jacket, a blue shirt and my skinny jeans. I fix my hair and I go back downstairs.

"You look nice, Jacko!" my mum says as I walk past the kitchen.

"Hmmm, you can't polish a turd though, can you?" I say back.

My mum laughs. "Don't be silly, love, they all know what you're going through, and you look great, they will just be happy to see you."

"Yeah, I suppose…"

I walk into my room and pour some more cider. I have a bit of time before I leave. My mum has agreed to give me a lift to the station. Getting a bus sounds like hell at the moment so I am very happy about this. I sit down and strum on my guitar a little bit.

I have been writing music whilst I've been this way. Although it seems everything I write just sounds terrible. I used to think my music was best when I was drunk/drinking, but this just isn't the case.

I put down my guitar and spark a cigarette. I feel okay at the moment.

I inhale and exhale deeply.

My mum hates me smoking in my room, so I try to do it by the window.

I turn and look in the mirror. I'm ready to go now and I go and check if my mum is ready. She says she is and she gives me a hug.

"Just make sure you are careful today love."

"I'll try my best, Mum…"

We leave and get in the car. I feel a jolt of adrenaline hit me; this is normal now, everything makes me nervous.

We get to the station with a bit of time to spare. I tell my mum I'm going to just wait on the platform. She gives me a hug and I say goodbye and leave the car.

It's a Saturday and it is very busy outside the station.

I wait until my mum is out of eyesight and I head towards a pub next to the station. I have about half an hour so I want to wait in somewhere that is safe for me. By this point pubs are like medication pit stops, so I feel at home here.

I enter and sit at the bar.

"How can I help, fella?"

"Double whiskey please, mate," I say.

"Starting early are we?" he says.

I want to tell him to fuck off and mind his business, but instead I laugh and say a line I've become accustomed to saying.

"It's six o'clock somewhere."

"Very true!" he says.

He passes me my drink and I drain it.

"Another one, please, pal."

"Sure."

He pours another and I get out my phone.

Twenty-five minutes until my train gets here. I feel excited now. It's gonna be great to see everyone. I haven't showed my face in a long time, most people know why. I suppose the fact I'm going into detox will help stop people worrying about me today.

"You all right to watch my stuff while I run to the toilet, mate?" I say to the bartender.

"No worries," he says.

I head towards the toilet and there is someone else in one of the cubicles and another man outside at the sink. I hear sniffing. They are talking loudly to each other. I recognise the man standing at the sink. He is a dealer of the powder variety.

"All right, buddy," I say.

"Do I know you?"

"Yeah, you sold to me and some mates of mine a while ago."

He looks aggressively at me. "Right, yeah I remember," he says, looking at me cautiously.

I head into the cubicle and hear him talking to his friend.

"Hurry up, mate, fucking hell."

His friend doesn't respond, he sniffs loudly from the cubicle next to mine.

I have a piss then leave the cubicle.

"Did you want anything?" he says to me.

"What have you got," I say.

"Charlie," he says.

"How much?" I say, washing my hands.

"Forty."

I don't know why I'm doing this. I used to do a bit of coke now and again but haven't in a long time.

"All right," I say. I take out two twenties from my wallet and he hands me a small see-through bag with white powder inside.

"You got my number still?" he says.

"Nah, I don't think so I got a new phone," I say taking out my phone.

I take his number and tell him I'll use him in the future if I need more.

I head back into the cubicle.

I empty a small amount onto the plastic toilet roll holder's casing.

Haven't done this in a while. I feel a bit anxious, maybe I shouldn't be doing this.

That thought goes as quickly as it came and I start pressing down on the rocks of cocaine to break it apart. I dice up the powder and form two white lines. I roll up a five pound note and sniff them both fast.

I put the baggie in a small pocket of my jeans and leave the cubicle.

"Take care, bud," I say.

"Yeah, safe, mate," he says.

I exit the toilet and head back to my stuff at the bar. I down the tumbler of whiskey and order another.

My head feels like all the blood has rushed to it. I feel my heart beat rapidly in my chest. I feel fucking fantastic. I drink some of the whiskey and look at my phone. Ten minutes until my train. I down my drink, order another, drink that and leave the bar.

I have a buzz now. I feel excited for the gig and to see my friends. I walk toward the station. Buy my ticket, and head towards the platform. There are a few people dotted about, but overall not massively busy. I sit down and roll a cigarette.

I spark it, take a drag and wait.

"It's illegal to smoke on platforms," says a man in a suit a couple of feet from me.

"How so?" I say.

"What do you mean how so? It's the law, mate, put it out," he says, looking at me in a very judgmental manner.

"Oh fuck off..." I say under my breath. He hears me.

"Sorry?" he says.

"I said fuck off. I don't know you, why are you even talking to me. Fuck off down that way and stop talking to me."

He looks at me a bit shocked. Shakes his head and says something under his breath I can't hear.

That was a bit out of character for me. I can feel my heart pulsing in my chest. I think for a second that it's most likely because of the coke that I got angry, but I dispel the thought from my mind. I have another drag of my cigarette and stub it out on the floor.

The train arrives on time and I stand up.

It pulls in and I board the door in front of me. It's very busy. I find a seat on its own near the back of the train and I sit.

I reach into my bag and pull out some headphones and a can of cider. I plug in my headphones and start listening to some music.

I had a girlfriend once who lived in London. This was just as my drinking had started getting bad, quite a while ago. I would often not have money and she would pay for me to come up to see her on the train. I would get pissed on my way up to London on the train and then drink when I got there.

I didn't treat her as well as I should have. I was selfish and cold and if I couldn't drink when I was with her I would be a nightmare to be around. I feel bad about this and I think about it for a second. I have to push this thought down because it's making me sad and I can't think about things like this right now. I put on some upbeat music and start drinking. It always helps me forget.

I shut my eyes and rest my head against the window.

I remember that I have coke in my pocket and get up. I leave my stuff on the seat and head to the toilet.

I open up the door. It fucking stinks. I find that toilets on trains are always the worst. I suppose the swaying and jolts of the train create disgusting accidents quite a lot within this toilet. I put the toilet seat down. I don't really have a surface I can sniff on in here. I get the baggie from my pocket, get out my house keys and stick the key into the bag. I pull out a small rock and I sniff it straight up my nose. I do this a couple of times. I can feel my throat going numb and can't feel my tongue anymore. Perfect.

I leave the toilet and Head back to my seat.

I feel fucking great. Slightly pissed and got a buzz that is making me smile.

I sit back down and start to drink more.

I look out the window and watch the haze of green, brown and grey flit past my window. I am a very nosey person so I like to look into people's houses and gardens as the train flies past.

You can kill quite a lot of time doing this, I have found.

The ticket man comes over to me and I show him my return ticket.

"Okay, lovely," he says as he holds it up.

"Thank you," I say.

I get a sudden thought. What if they have checks at the gate of the gig? They most likely will. This freaks me out. I could put the baggie down my pants I suppose. They wouldn't check in my pants, would they? Shit, I don't know.

I get up and head back to the toilet and repeat the process with my keys and coke.

Maybe if I do the whole thing before I get there? That's quite a lot though and may ruin the day. Or make the day amazing? No. I'll just put it in my pants or somewhere else when I get there.

The train pulls into London Bridge and I get off. I head towards the entrance of the station for a cigarette. I get outside and I spark up. There is a busker near the entrance and I stand listening to him play guitar. He is good.

The sun has broken through the clouds now and I stand with my eyes shut listening to the music with the warmth on my face. I smoke and listen.

I finish my cigarette and head over to the man playing guitar and put five pounds in the basket sitting in front of him.

"Thank you, my man!" he says.

"My pleasure, buddy, keep it up!" I say.

I used to busk a lot in Tunbridge Wells. I know what it's like. It's fun but it does get tiring and you just want people to listen. A lot of the time people are just trying to get to where they need to be. Occasionally someone will stop and listen and that makes it all worthwhile.

I head back inside the station and approach someone who works there.

"Excuse me, what train do I need to get to get to Hyde Park?"

"No problem, get the tube to Green Park station on the Jubilee line, then to Knightsbridge station, Piccadilly," he says smiling.

"Thank you, mate!" I say walking fast towards the underground.

"No worries! I'd just follow the crowd to be honest, mate!"

He's right quite a few people wearing merch of my friend's band are heading in the same direction as we.

I get down into the underground and it's heaving. I always find it hard to breathe down here. Its air always feels thick and soupy, and used. It makes me feel sick but I put that to the back of my mind and head towards the platform I need.

I stand on the platform and see a seat available near to me. I go over and sit down. I use my Jacket to cover my face and I take some more coke, making sure no one can see me. I look mental, but I would rather look mental then be doing coke when everyone can see me.

I open another can of cider and wait for my train. I feel eyes on me. I look round and notice a dirty look from a family standing on the platform. I ignore it, I can't really blame them. Usually this type of thing would upset me but I'm buzzing and couldn't give a shit.

My train arrives and I board. There is nowhere to sit so I stand, squeezed up against strangers in a hot sticky herd. We sway to and fro as the train crashes along and I feel claustrophobic. I shut my eyes again.

We arrive and I get off. I board my next tube which is less busy and head towards the destination. I arrive and follow a group of teenagers headed towards the park.

I catch a look at myself in the reflection of a car window and notice I have powder around my nose. Now I know what the dirty look was for. I wipe it off and rub it into my gums. I look like a ghost in the reflection. My eyes are so sunken and I look dead.

Oh well.

I reach the park and before I head towards the entrance I put my baggie in my pants. I head towards the gate and pull out my phone. I show my e-ticket and my bag is checked. They see cider inside but say nothing. I am let in and I call my friends on my phone.

They answer.

"Hey where are you?" I say loudly.

"We are near the middle! Didn't want to be close to the front as too many people!"

"Okay, mate, I'm on my way." I hang up.

I walk for around five minutes and finally find them. A lot of the same faces from the previous gig I went to are here as well as others who I haven't seen for a long time. I run over and hug my friend.

"Jackooo!" Dan says and hugs me tight.

"Hey, buddy, sorry I'm late, what time did you all get here?"

"About an hour ago man, it's all good, don't worry!"

I sit down on the grass and say my hellos to the other people there. The gig has started already but Isaac hasn't been on yet.

"The Libertines are up next."

"Oh really?" I say. In all honesty I haven't even looked at the line-up. I just agreed to come and didn't really think much about why.

I pull out the baggie from my pants and key a small amount into my nose. No one sees me do this and I put it back into my pocket.

I feel a burning ache in my lower back and in my stomach. I ignore it and talk to my friends. I tell them about detox, about things that have happened this past month and how happy I am to be getting help.

"But you're drinking now…" says one of my friends.

"I know, I have to drink until I get there, otherwise I will withdraw," I say.

"Fuck that sounds horrible," she says.

"It is…"

There is a very beautiful girl here. I've known her a while and we had a drunken thing once. It is still awkward between us. I smile at her, she smiles back.

I've heard that she has asked about me and how I've been doing. I don't read too much into it, as she could just be being friendly.

"Hey, Jack," she says.

"Hey."

"How are you? I haven't seen you for ages…"

"I know, I've been off the radar for a while, not been too well."

"I heard…"

"Yeah, it's been pretty rough. I go into detox in a few days."

"I heard that too."

"Oh right," I say.

"Are you scared?" she says.

"I am. I am excited though. I just want to feel better now."

"I can imagine." She smiles.

"Anyway, I'll catch up with you in a bit," I say, nervously taking a sip of my drink.

"Yeah, okay, good to see you, Jack." She hugs me.

"You too," I reply.

The aching in my lower back is still there. I also feel like I've been punched in the gut. It's a dull ache, and it makes me feel sick.

I head towards the portable toilets and I enter.

I take out the cocaine and I empty some of the packet onto my wallet and make three lines. I snort it up and I turn to the toilet.

This feeling in my stomach hurts, I don't feel great.

I open the toilet seat and I am sick violently into it.

Blood sprays on the bottom of the plastic. Not good. It's never been that much blood.

I wipe my mouth clean and I exit the toilet. I feel sick still. My stomach aches and my head hurts.

I drink some more and try to ignore it. I head back to my friends and I realise that the next band is on. I am a big fan and my friends invite me with them to get closer, I decline and sit down where I was, on my own.

I push my hand into my stomach to try to find the source of the pain.

It's sitting underneath my left rib cage. It's so painful.

I daydream on the spot. I feel dizzy and sick.

I drink more and try to forget the pain.

An hour or so passes and I realise I can taste blood in my mouth.

I get up and feel panicked.

"I've got to go," I say to my friend.

"What? Isaac's not even been on yet!"

"I have to go, mate, I'm not well."

My friend looks at me concerned but says goodbye and heads over to the front of the heaving body of people watching the gig. I don't say goodbye to anyone else, I just leave.

I can't believe this is fucking happening again.

I pass by people entering the gig and I walk out of the gates. I head to the nearest toilet and I enter. I sit on the toilet seat with my head against the door crying.

Everything hurts now.

I leave and I head to an off license and pick up a bottle of vodka. I leave, open it and drink a quarter of it. It burns but I don't care. If I'm drunk I won't care.

I head towards the tube station and I board a train headed for London Bridge. I drink and shut my eyes on the tube. I just want to be home now.

At least I won't withdraw. At least that can't happen.

I get off the train and walk up a steep hill towards London Bridge. Every part of me is aching. My legs feel like jelly and my stomach and lower back are on fire.

I go to climb some stairs.

I trip and I fall.

I hit my head on the cold concrete. I try to push myself up and someone grabs my arm.

"Are you okay?"

A man has me steady and is holding my arm, looking concerned.

"Thank you. I am okay, sorry, thank you, I'm okay," I say, lifting myself up and releasing my arm from his grip.

"Are you sure? You hit your head, are you sure you're okay?" he says, a very worried look on his face.

"I'm fine, thank you, I appreciate it but I'm fine." I walk as fast as I can away from the situation. He stands motionless in the same spot I fell. I don't feel embarrassed, I feel sick, and I don't have time to care about this.

I head towards the boards that inform the public which trains are at which platforms. I find the right train and I board it. I find a seat on my own and I close my eyes.

My mind is racing and I feel fucking dreadful.

I think about all of my friends at the park and I feel so sad. I feel jealous that I can't be there, and I feel like I have let my friend down.

I get up and go to the toilet. I drink half of the bottle of vodka. I want to be sick as I drink but I don't let myself. I keep draining it. I want to not think anymore. I don't want to feel.

I head back to my seat and I close my eyes again. I wait for the train to leave. I let it rock me to sleep as I doze in and out of consciousness. I feel sleepy. I have to make sure I wake up in time. I set a timer on my phone for half an hour and I close my eyes. I sleep.

I wake up to my phone blaring in my pocket and realise I'm one stop away from where I get off. My head is splitting and I am shaking.

I take out the bottle of vodka in my inside pocket and drink the rest. It burns my throat. I check my phone and I have a missed call from my mum.

I message her and ask her to pick me up from the station in ten minutes. My stomach no longer feels as bad as it was. My shaking already has subsided and my heart has calmed. I take out my cider from my bag and start drinking.

The carriage is pretty empty, apart from a few people. I need a cigarette badly.

As the train pulls into my station, I wonder whether I have drink at home. I don't. I get off the train, head out of the station and go to the nearest off license. I pick up a small bottle of whiskey and eight cans of cider and load it into my bag.

"Big night?" says the man behind the counter.

I don't respond. I walk out. I'm not explaining my drinking right now to a stranger.

I go and sit at the bus stop outside the station and open the whiskey. I drink. I spark up a cigarette. I smoke, I exhale.

My mum messaged while I was on the train and I get her text late.

'Meet me in the car park love x'

I get up and walk round the station to the car park and spot my mum's car. I walk over. She looks happy. I don't really want to spoil that.

I get in the car.

"Hi, love! How was it? You're back early? Did you start feeling ill?" she says, hugging me as I put on my seatbelt.

"Yeah you could say that, I didn't even get to watch him play," I say.

"Oh no, I'm sorry, love, that's awful. Well at least you came back and didn't stay up there and get worse."

"Yeah, I suppose," I say. "I don't feel that great if I'm honest, Mum, I was sick when I was there and my lower back and stomach have been hurting a lot."

My mum looks sad.

"Well that's not surprising, with the way your body is at the moment," she says.

She's right. What do I expect. I drink way more than I need to and I wonder why I'm sick and my liver hurts. I don't tell her about the rest of the trip, I don't want to upset her.

I already feel a lot better to be honest. Sitting here knowing that I am going home and it's safe there, makes me feel good.

We get home after a ten minute car ride and I get out of the car and head towards the house. My mum gets out and approaches the door. I hug her.

"Thank you, Mum, I can't wait until this is all over."

"I know, Jacko, I know, me too."

We go inside and I head into my room and sit down. I remember I have the coke in my pocket. I get up. Go over to the toilet and flush it. I don't want it now. I have a couple of days until I leave and I don't want to fuck myself up so badly I can't even get there.

I go back into my room and pick up my phone. I message Isaac telling him why I left and that I am sorry. I do feel awful about not staying. There are thousands of people there, though, he wouldn't have missed me.

I switch on the TV and start watching. I feel knackered. I feel very weak and tired. I may just go to bed.

I pour myself a cider and drink. I go back to the sofa and lie down. I shut my eyes. I'm so exhausted. I go through all the events of the day in my head. Like watching a film back in first person.

It was going so well. I guess I shouldn't beat myself up about it, at least I got out of the house. I'm glad I made an effort. I think about the kind man who helped me up when I fell. It makes me feel better about the human race slightly.

The thing is I always think people just think I look mad or disgusting. Maybe there are people out there who just want to help, who see a person falling and want to do anything they can to get them back up again.

I hope one day I am the person helping someone back up, and not falling.

That would be nice.

Chapter 13: Preparations

Today is my last full day of drinking. Tomorrow I will leave for detox. I will hand over my old life in exchange for a new one. I woke up today after an hour's sleep.

The familiar shaking was there. I pushed myself to the edge of my bed and used the wall for support to stand because my legs shook so badly, and I headed downstairs and I started drinking. That was at four a.m.

It is now ten a.m. I have received letters in the post from members of my family wishing me good luck. My friends have all wished me well and are excited to know the new me.

I cry at some of the letters I receive.

I can see a true smile on my mum's face, the first in a long time. My brother seems happier and so does my mum's fiancé Phil. I have spoken to my dad on the phone and he wished me well, reminding me he is proud of me and that he loves me very much. I love him for this.

My mum and dad divorced when I was two years old. After that I saw my dad every Sunday. We stopped speaking for a while. I think due to the fact I was pushing back against my parents. Unfortunately, my dad didn't live with me so when I pushed back against him, it wasn't so easy to make up. He has always done his best for me, and always shown support in anything in life I wanted to do, the same can be said about my mum. I cry when I read his message and speak to him on the phone and I appreciate it more then he will ever know.

Phil has been supporting my mum throughout this. He has been with her for around twenty years, and I don't know what she would have done if not for him. We haven't always seen eye to eye, but I haven't been an easy person to be around a lot of the time. I hope after this, things will be different.

My mum comes in and tells me that we have to go out in a while to pick me up some new pyjamas for detox. I tell her I don't mind my old ones. She disagrees and tells me I should have new ones. I don't fight this at all, as all my clothes are pretty old anyway.

My mum leaves the house for a while to ride her horse. She has a horse called Alfie and a Shetland pony called Sprout. They are down the road at some stables my mum rents. I don't know why people always think that people who have horses must be rich. Because we aren't at all. My mum has always dreamed of riding horses. She grew up in London (as did my dad) and she always dreamed of one day leaving London and being able to ride horses in the country. She achieved this through hard work and determination.

I wish I wasn't this way and I wish things came to me easier and life didn't confuse me so much. It does though, and I am going to try to do better. She deserves better, my family deserve better.

I go in the kitchen and eat my daily piece of toast. It still makes me sick if I eat too much. I can't wait to eat a massive meal. I can't wait to cook, go out to eat, maybe even take someone out to eat one day.

I think the 'taking someone out to eat' is a bit farfetched but it's a nice image.

I still can't get over the thought that I will be better. This has become so routine.

No sleep, drink, throw up, drink, throw up, drink, bed. Every day for what feels like an eternity.

I think when this is over I want to help people like myself. I've always seen myself as a musician, but I'm starting to think maybe I understood music and just assumed that was my thing. I can't bear the thought of there being others out there like myself. Alone, helpless and scared. So many aren't as lucky as I am. So many don't have a family support network or even a home.

It hurts to think about. I think I'm running before I can walk. I should focus on getting myself clean and if things work out then maybe think of that as an option.

I have a million and one thoughts in my head, all the time. I can never focus. My whole life I feel like I have been swimming against the tide. Fighting tooth and nail against my own head and trying to figure out how to be normal and what normal is.

I hope they can answer these questions for me.

When I started drinking it was fun. I would play gigs, maybe get free drink, if not bring my own and it was always great. I don't really know when things went wrong. I guess it was when I started to use it to make life more exciting and interesting. Not that it did, but everything seems great when you are drunk, or it did with me for the most part.

I have come to realise that my body is just not cut out for it anymore. There is something broken deep inside and until I fix that I will forever be chasing the numb bliss I experienced at the beginning.

I head out. I walk to the shop and pick up some whiskey and some strong cider.

I like how whiskey feels when it hits my stomach. The pain lets me know it's working.

I walk back home. On my way back, I stop in a field on the road leading to my house.

I sit down and I roll a cigarette. I spark up, drink half the whiskey and sit.

I look out over the field. It slopes down into a forest. I look into the horizon. I can see the motorway in the distance and a ton of woodland surrounding it. I think about how different things could have been. I think about all the paths that led to here, me sitting on this bench right now.

Life is incredible but ferocious. It's a playground full of cavernous potholes and it's unforgiving. You have to make sure you take the right steps or fall down into abyss.

I head back to mine and I go into my room. It's evening now and I decide to watch some YouTube videos on what to expect when I get to detox. It doesn't really help as it's all American and things are very different over here.

I give up.

I watch a film instead. I pour myself a tumbler of whiskey and a pint of cider. I down the cider then sink the whiskey. I feel good today. I think knowing that this is the last time I will go to sleep drunk is helping.

My mum arrives back home and spots the whiskey through my bedroom window (my bedroom is the bottom floor facing the drive). She shakes her head. Shit. I didn't really want her to see that.

She comes into my room.

"Whiskey, Jack? Really?"

"Yeah, it's my last night of drinking, Mum, I just fancied it."

She makes a disapproving face and walks out of my room. I follow her.

"What do I need to pack, Mum?"

"Well you will be there around 12 days so just clothes for lounging and some everyday clothes, your toothbrush etcetera," she says.

"Okay, will do. When are we going out to get my stuff?"

"In about ten minutes so make sure you're ready."

"Okay," I say. I head back to my room, get my Jacket on, put my whiskey in my inside pocket. I wait for my mum and she comes downstairs and tells me she is ready to go.

We head towards a supermarket chain that sells standard clothing. I'm not a big fan of shopping. I hate the whole walking around slowly looking at stuff routine. Luckily, it's only PJs we are getting so I think it should be a pretty quick shop.

We enter and I notice there aren't many people. Thank god.

We walk towards an aisle full of men's and women's clothing.

"Is it just pyjamas I'm getting?" I ask.

"Well if you see anything else that you like, plain white T-shirts or something, let me know."

"Okay," I say.

We find the aisle full of men's T-shirts and pyjamas. I am really nervous about tomorrow now. I don't know why but this is making it all real. It's just been an idea or a suggestion for so long. I never actually thought I would be lucky enough to actually go.

I pick out what I need and some extra bits like plain T-shirts. We head to the counter and pay. I'm getting a few funny looks. I can't wait until this shit is a thing of the past. I only ever want people looking at me if they have a good reason in the future, not because I look like a walking corpse.

We leave and my mum offers to get me a McDonalds. I decline but thank her for the offer. I still can't eat fucking anything.

I don't know why but I start feeling very emotional.

"Mum, I just want to say how much I appreciate everything you have done for me. I wouldn't be here without you and I owe you my life."

My mum smiles as she drives.

"Don't be silly, Jacko, I'm your mum, and it's my job to look out for you," she says.

"You shouldn't have to do all you have done though, it isn't normal for me to put you through so much, I'm sorry."

My mum smiles again. "Tomorrow is the start of your new life, love, finally."

"I know, I can't wait, I'm so nervous though. I'm going to be on my own for the first time in so long and I am scared," I say.

"I know, but you won't be alone, Jack. There is twenty-four staff and you will be in the safest place possible!"

"Yeah, I guess," I say. She is right. It's normal for me to be nervous. It's a huge thing. I just need to put all my faith and trust in them, and let them do what they do best, get people clean.

We get home and I head back into my room. I finish off my whiskey and start packing stuff into a luggage bag. I pack the letters I was given by my loved ones. I pack a couple of books, I don't really read but I pack them anyway in case I get bored or need a distraction.

I pack my new clothes and I also pack a couple of pouches of tobacco I picked up. Thank god they allow smoking, giving up cigarettes as well as alcohol would be beyond difficult.

I pack a dressing gown and my toiletries. I zip up the case and I stand it by my door. I feel so anxious now. I need to calm down. I open a can of cider and I pour it into a glass. I drink. I sit and I watch the rest of my film.

In twenty-four hours I will be without alcohol.

Fuck.

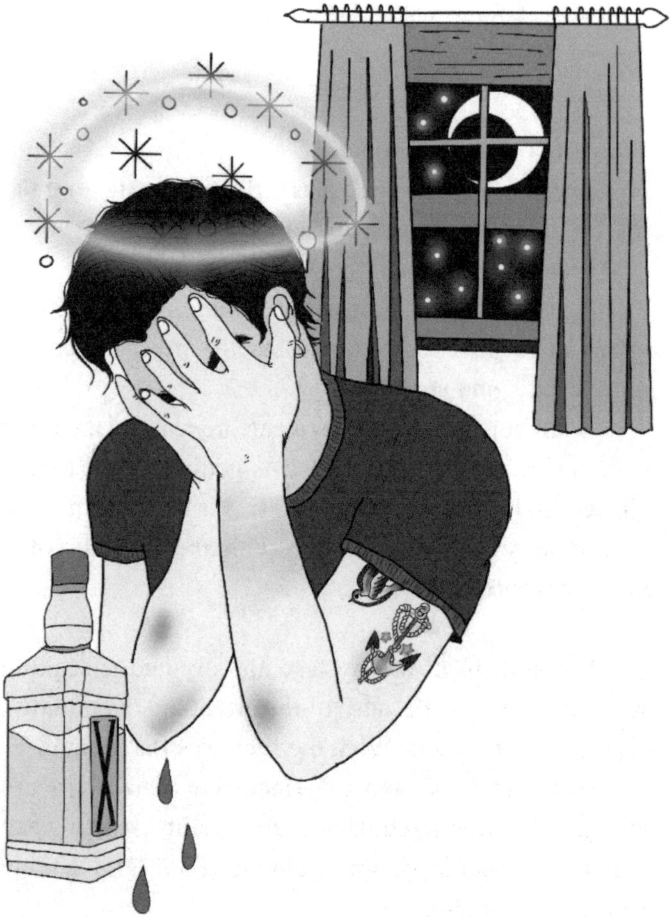

Chapter 14: New start

I'm in a bright white room.

There is a small back mass, floating in the middle. It is writhing, contorting and vibrating.

I feel danger emanating from it.

It grows larger and smaller. It emits a low hum, a growl. The growl gets louder as the object becomes more erratic and unstable.

Loud bursts of sound permeate my ears as the mass gets bigger. I can't escape it. It is getting closer to me. Closer and more threatening. It shrinks down to a miniscule size then explodes with the ferocity of a nuclear bomb.

I wake.

Sweat drips down my face and my bed is soaking wet. I assume it is because of the sweat but soon realise I have pissed myself. What the fuck was that dream.

I've had it on and off since this started. In my childhood it was a regular occurrence, it used to wake me in the middle of the night, terrified. It's getting worse now though.

I get up. I change my sheets and flip the bed. I feel disgusting. I haven't ever pissed myself before. Since

I've been abusing drink it's become something that occasionally happens. It never gets less shameful.

I check my phone and see it is five a.m. I managed to get some sleep, that's all that matters.

I head into the kitchen and I get a bottle of cider. I head back into my bedroom and pour myself pint after pint until my withdrawal settles down.

I run to the toilet and I am sick. The drink I just ingested is sprayed back out again. It's okay. I'm used to this. I flush the toilet and head back into my room and start drinking more. My stomach usually stays settled for a short time after I am sick the first time, so I know I can drink again. I smoke a cigarette and look out the window into the night.

Oh my god. I don't know how but I completely forgot about today. A jolt of anxiety surges through me and I start to panic.

I look around my room and check I have everything ready. I do. I remember I was told to drink as usual just until I get there, so I feel myself calm down slightly.

I hear my mum get up. She walks down the stairs and spots my light on.

She knocks and comes in.

"You okay, Jacko? Today's the day!" she says, smiling excitably.

"I know, I'm so nervous."

"Well that's natural. It will be okay, love. Just think, you will be out of this nightmare soon."

"I know. I can't wait but I'm scared."

"Don't be scared, darling. It's going to be okay. I'm heading out to do the horses but when I get back make sure you are ready as we have to be there by ten a.m."

I nod.

"Sure."

"Chin up, love," my mum says, she exits as she leaves. I see her drive off in her car. She must be so relieved. I am, but for her it must be so good to know her son won't be killing himself anymore. He will be healthy and will be getting better.

I stub out my cigarette and head upstairs to the shower.

I shave. I splash moisturiser on my face with water and I get into the shower.

I wash, get dried and exit.

I head downstairs and I get changed into some comfy clothes. I guess they won't mind if I wear these to the facility. Surely.

I send a message to Isaac. It's early but he will see it when he wakes up. I tell him today's the day, and that I look forward to seeing him when I'm better. I say thank you to him for his support. I send a similar message to my sister, my dad and a couple of others.

I sit down and continue drinking. I drink until my mum comes home and I keep drinking while she gets ready.

I go upstairs and see my brother and Phil and give them hugs.

They wish me well and tell me they are proud of me. I appreciate this. My mum tells me she will be ready in a few minutes, so I head back downstairs and take out my remaining cider from the fridge.

"Do you have the postcode, Mum?" I shout upstairs.

"No, can you get it from the paperwork?" she shouts back.

I head into my room and retrieve the sheet of paper with directions printed on it.

I stuff it into my Jacket pocket and head into the hall with my luggage and my cider. I wait here for my mum. I am nervous and I can't relax. I roll a cigarette and head outside and smoke it fast. I need to calm down. I need to remember why I am doing this. I'm fucking terrified. What if I die while I'm in there? Stop fucking thinking that Jack. This place is safe and it's the best place for me.

I chuck my cigarette and roll another. I smoke it just as fast. I hear my mum coming down the stairs and she asks if I'm ready, smiling and looking proud.

"I am," I say, terrified.

I grab my bag and my cider from the hall and I walk to the car and get in. I take out the sheet of paper with directions on it and put it on my lap. I open my cider and down a quarter of it.

I swallow and I repeat. This is the last time I can drink, I'm going to make sure I drink it all.

My mum gets in the car and she starts it up. We leave and I wave to Ben and Phil from the car.

We make our way towards Maidstone. That is where the detox unit is located. I turn on the radio and me and my mum sit and listen to it for a while.

"Are you okay, love?" my mum asks.

"I'm scared shitless, Mum. I know I have to do this but I'm so scared." I can feel myself getting upset.

"I know, love, but honestly it isn't going to be for that long and when you leave you will have your life back."

"Yeah, I know, thanks, I know I just need to remind myself of that," I say, rubbing my face in my hands. I open my cider and down half. I have another bottle with me, my last bottle before I stop for good. I also have a can of very strong cider in my Jacket pocket. I'll have that just before I get there. That will hopefully stop any withdrawals for a while.

We drive through country roads, motorways and villages. We go past places I have never seen before, places that seem like they are trapped in time. I gaze out the window watching the scenery pass by.

"Oh shit," my mum says, looking very concerned at the sat nav.

"What?" I say.

"I think we are lost."

"How can we be lost when we have sat nav?" I say. I am panicking now. If I'm going there, I want to go there, not get lost and end up somewhere else.

"I know, love..." My mum starts panicking too and takes another road in the wrong direction.

"Mum, fucking hell how can we be lost? I don't need this today! Of all fucking days!" I feel myself getting angry and I know the anger is misplaced. It isn't really directed at my mum it is just nerves, but in this moment, she gets the brunt of it.

"Jack, I am trying my best, I'm sorry, we will be fine."

Fuck. I've made her cry. She is wiping tears from her face while she frantically tries to get us back on track.

"Hang on, no wait, let's just pull over."

My mum nods and pulls over into a side lane.

I reach over and I hug her.

"I'm sorry, Mum, I didn't mean to snap at you, I am just really nervous. You're doing your best, it's in the middle of nowhere!"

She nods and wipes tears from her eyes. "I just know how much today means to you, and I of all people want to get you there on time," she says.

God, I feel awful.

"Please don't worry about it, we will get there when we get there. I love you and thank you for being so amazing and taking me today." I hug her again and she looks slightly happier.

"I love you too, Jacko, I was just panicking then for a second," she says.

She starts the car and we resume trying to find this detox facility, which feels like it may as well be in Middle-fucking-Earth.

We drive for what feels like forever. We pull into a side road, with a dirt track leading down a country path. We follow the path and I realise we have arrived.

"Wait a second," I say to my mum.

I pull out my last can of cider. I open it and I drink all of it as fast as I can. I wait a second and roll a cigarette and smoke. I need a minute. This is making me panic. I take a few deep breaths.

"It's going to be okay, Jacko," my mum says, placing a hand on my back.

"Yeah, I know, I'll be okay." I have to be strong now. Not just for me but for my mum. I can't go anywhere and this is it. It's here. Sobriety and healthy living is within feet and I need to grasp it.

"Okay, let's go," I say.

My mum pulls into the car park. There is an old disused barn to our right with old chairs stacked inside. To our left is the facility. I say facility, it looks more like a hotel, a nice country hotel. It has two oast towers on each end. There are a few steps leading up to the front door, which has glass panels. I can see into the reception.

My mum looks at me with a hopeful smile and we get out.

I walk to the back of the car, grab my luggage from the boot and we walk up the steps to the detox.

We sound the buzzer.

The door clicks and another buzzer sounds. We push the door open, head inside and stand in the reception.

It is a small room with a crescent shaped desk facing the door. There are two chairs to our left as we walk in. We sit down. A woman enters into the room.

"Hello! You must be Jack!" She has electric red hair, with a black top and black jeans on. Her name tag says:

BRIDGE HOUSE STAFF:
LYNNE

"Hello," I say quietly.

"Hi there!" my mum responds.

"My name is Lynne and I'm a recovery worker here, Jack, how are you doing today?" She smiles down at me.

"I'm not too bad, quite weak," I say.

A man enters the room. He has black hair, is quite small and is wearing a shirt and tie with black fitted trousers.

"Hello, Jack, my name is Tom." He shakes me and my mum's hand.

"You must be his long suffering mother," he says smiling.

My mum smiles back. "I am, hello, I think we spoke on the phone," she replies.

"We did," he says. He has a southern Irish accent. "Okay, Jack what I'm going to need you to do is say your goodbyes to your mum and we can take you through to be inducted. Have you had something to eat? Lynne, can you grab something to eat for Jack here?" He looks at Lynne.

"Of course, Jack, do you like chicken?" she says, looking down, smiling.

"Um, I do, I'm not sure I can eat though. I haven't been able to," I say. This is all moving very fast and I feel extremely panicked.

"No problem, Jack, you can just eat what you like, nothing or anything, it's fine," Tom says. "We will be back in a minute, Jack, so I will give you five minutes with your mum to say goodbye, okay?" He walks into another room with Lynne and I turn to my mum.

"I'm scared, Mum." My heart is pounding in my chest.

My mum looks at me and looks very hopeful. "This is it, Jacko. I'm so proud of you and I will speak to you in a couple of days, okay? I know it is scary but just keep telling yourself why you are here. This isn't a punishment, it is to give you a new life."

I start to cry. "I know, I'm sorry I'm just so nervous." I hug my mum and we both stand up.

"Trust me, this will go quicker than you think. Relax, enjoy getting better and remember we are all so proud of you."

I release my mum. "I know, okay, I know I can do this," I say, breathing slowly.

"You can, love, I know you can," she replies.

Tom enters the room and addresses my mum. "Okay, are we all set? We will take good care of him, Sue, don't worry," He says looking at me. I try to smile but feel so scared.

"Okay, I'm sure you will, thank you so much," my mum says.

"No problem at all. Now you get home and get some much needed sleep," he says. They both laugh and I hug my mum once more.

"I love you, see you soon," I say.

"Love you too, Jacko, I'll speak to you in a couple of days, okay?"

My mum leaves.

I sit down and Tom explains to me that he will be back in a few moments. He asks me how much I've had to drink and I tell him. He writes it down on a note pad and exits.

Lynne enters the room and puts a hot plate of chicken with mash potato and vegetables on a table next to me.

"Here you go, Jack. Enjoy!" she says. She too leaves the room and I am left on my own.

I feel sick. I can't eat. My heart it pumping hard in my chest. I am boiling hot and I am shaking. I'm terrified. I don't have my support here. My mum is gone. It's just me and them now. I have to do this. I have to make this work.

I put a small piece of chicken in my mouth and try to chew.

My mouth is so dry. I can't even taste what I am eating. I swallow and decide not to eat another bite.

Tom returns with a file in his hands.

"Okay, Jack? Have you managed to eat anything?"

"I can't eat any more at the moment. I had a bit of chicken," I say.

"That's fine, well at least you had something," he says.

Lynne enters with a camera.

"Jack, would you mind if we took your picture for our files? Also so you can look back on it when you leave."

"Sure," I say.

She holds the camera still and the flash goes off.

"Thanks, Jack," she says.

"No problem," I say.

"Jack, if you want to follow me, leave that food there, someone will come and grab it in a minute. We are going through here to do your induction," Tom says, motioning to the doors to my left.

"Okay," I say. I get up and walk with Tom through the doors. As I walk through I see the living room to my left. There is a very large stone fireplace, a big television, a couple of sofas and at the far end, a huge table that seats around twenty people.

"Okay, just in here, Jack." Tom shows me to a door and I walk into a games room.

There is a pool table, table football and a large number of chairs propped up against the wall of the circular room.

I see there is a makeshift desk in front of the entrance, three chairs and a singular chair for me in front of the desk. I go and sit down.

Two others enter after me. One is a very muscular man with glasses and grey hair and another is Lynne.

Tom, the man I don't know and Lynne sit down and start to look at their files.

"So, Jack, do you know why you are here today?"

"Yes," I say.

"Why is that?"

"To get better."

"And do you want to get better?"

"Yes, but I am scared."

Tom nods his head and Lynne smiles sympathetically.

"Well, Jack it would be strange if you weren't scared, wouldn't it? This is something completely different to your everyday life. The way you live at the moment is a routine and this is breaking your routine, isn't it?" Tom says. He speaks very fast and matter of fact. It makes me panicked but I feel I trust his judgment and also get the impression he knows what he is talking about.

"The reason we haven't put you into the main part of the house yet is because you have been drinking and our residents are in the process of detox so you can't be around them just yet," he says.

"Yeah, that makes sense," I say.

I look down at my hands, they are bright red and sweating.

"So why do you want to be here, Jack?" Tom says.

"I need to get better," I say. I feel tears coming. "If I don't get better I will die, and it's ruining mine and my family's life." Fuck I don't want to cry.

I can't help it. Tears begin streaming down my face. I can't breathe. I break down. I am alone in this place and I'm scared.

"I have to do this. I have to. Every part of me is screaming to get out, go home, and be around people that I know. I'm destroying my mum's life. I'm killing myself every day and I..." I am fully sobbing now. "Sorry, I can't breathe.," I say. My throat is closing up and I feel dizzy.

"Jack, it's okay. Just breathe, okay? It's all right you're in a safe place," Tom says.

Lynne comes over to me and hands me a glass of water. I lift it to my mouth, shaking violently.

"I can see how much you want this, Jack. Your poor mum was in tears on the phone to me, begging for you to come in as she believed you were going to die at home, so we moved you up the list. It wasn't easy though!"

I look up, still crying, I can't control it. "I didn't know that. I know I have to be here. Every part of me is screaming to leave right now but I have to do this. I have to get better."

"Well, you have the right attitude, Jack," Tom says. "I can see you want to get better."

Tom proceeds to look through the files in front of him. He begins asking me questions about how much I drink a day, how much I drank today, and in general how things have been. I tell him everything.

I am given a breathalyser. I am told that I will have to stay in my room for a while until the alcohol has left my system. I am told I will be given some Librium and vitamins to help stop withdrawal.

"You will be free of alcohol dependency when you leave here, Jack," Tom says. "Whether you stay clean? We can't control that, that's up to you."

I nod these; tears won't stop. "I know I need this, I'm sorry, I'm just so scared," I say.

"Well as I said this is a scary situation for you, but you are in great hands."

Tom introduces the man in the middle of him and Lynne. His name is Mike. He will be looking after my medication and administering it. He will also be around a lot if I need anyone to talk to.

"Good to meet you, mate," Mike says, smiling. He has a very kind face.

"Nice to meet you," I say. I'm still fucking crying.

"Okay, Jack so what we will do now is show you to your room. Once you're settled in, Mike will come to find you and start your medication, okay?" Tom says standing up.

I stand up and shake his hand.

"Honestly, thank you so much, I'm sorry I can't Thank you enough…"

"Jack, don't mention it. It's going to be all right, okay?" he says returning my hand shake.

I nod my head and smile.

I shake hands with Mike and Lynne.

I follow Mike out of the room and he leads me up a set of stairs next to the living room. It has a stairlift and it winds up to the left in the shape of a U. We get to the top of the stairs and turn left. There are a number of rooms down a long corridor.

We proceed down the corridor and Mike points out the toilets, shower and medical room.

"At night we ask that you keep your door ajar slightly. With a slipper or something, as we need to check on you every half an hour," he says.

"That's fantastic," I say. It really is. I was so worried I would just be left to myself and my messed up sleep at night. Knowing someone will be checking on me to make sure I'm okay makes me feel so much better.

"Yeah, we find people struggle and need some help the first few nights. If you ever need anyone at any time in the night, all you do is head to the medical office and knock. There is someone there day and night and if you are struggling to sleep or withdrawals are getting too bad, you go to them and they can relieve the symptoms, or give you something to help you sleep," Mike says.

He is walking in front of me and opens a door about midway down the corridor.

"This is you, mate," he says.

We both walk into the room. It is relatively small but pretty nice. It reminds me of a hotel room. There is a whiteboard and marker on the wall, a cupboard and a single bed near the bedroom door.

There is a small light above the bed, and a larger light in the middle of the room.

There is a small window with a nice view of a field opposite.

"Thank you."

"Not bad eh?" he says.

"Yeah," I say.

"Okay, mate, so if you come with me we can give you some Librium to help with the withdrawals and then you will have to wait in your room for a while until the alcohol gets out of your system," he says.

I leave my bags on the floor of my room and follow Mike into the hall. He heads towards a door with a padlock on it. He puts in the key and opens it up. We walk into a very small room. It smells strongly of hospitals. It's freezing. The light is very bright and Mike asks me to sit myself down on a chair next to the door.

I do this and he proceeds to unlock a cupboard, which I assume has medication inside. He pours a small amount of water into a paper cup and hands me the medication. I can't get it in me fast enough.

By this point I am withdrawing pretty bad. I am hearing things that aren't there. I know that isn't real and will pass when I start the medication.

I feel better almost immediately.

I'm sure it's a lot to do with my mind but I don't care. I start to feel better.

"While we are here, Jack, do you mind if we find out your weight and height? I also need to take a small amount of blood," he says.

"I don't mind," I say.

He directs me to some scales and begins taking my measurements.

"Sixteen stone two, in case you were wondering," he says, smiling.

"I am surprised I even weigh that, I haven't eaten in forever," I say.

"Yeah but you are quite a tall lad as well," he says. He fiddles with a contraption to tell how tall I am. "Aaaand six-foot-four." He looks at me surprised. "Cor, that is tall." He laughs and I laugh too.

"Yeah, I've always been pretty tall," I say.

I get off the scales and sit back down.

Mike puts a rubber strap around my arm, taps the vein a few times and extracts blood into a small glass vial. He removes the needle and puts a cotton bud on the area.

"So are you glad you're here finally," Mike says.

"I am, as I said, I am terrified but I have to do this. Not just for me but my family."

"Yeah, you're mum is very supportive, you have a great attitude to this, Jack. I have seen a lot of people come in with the wrong attitude, the way you are thinking is good," he says.

This makes me feel better. My hands aren't shaking as much anymore.

"Okay, all done," he says.

We leave and Mike leads me to my room.

"Okay, Jack, someone will be up to breathalyse you again in about half an hour."

"Okay, thank you Mike," I say.

"No problem, Jack, maybe unpack your bits and get yourself settled in. Back in a bit."

I sit down on my bed. I think about my mum, about home, about drink.

I start to cry. I miss home.

I bury my head in my pillow and wail into it. I have so much sadness inside, it's clawing at my chest, screaming to get out.

I scream and cry more into my pillow.

I hope no one can hear me. I don't really care, to be honest. It feels fucking good to cry.

I have to do this, I have to fucking do this.

I lie on my back and stare into the ceiling. I see faint outlines of phantoms dancing on the pale blank wall. I shut my eyes. I breathe in deep and exhale. This will pass. I have to do this. I have to be strong. I get up and shake violently. I throw up into a bin in the corner of my room. My stomach is killing me. I feel hot and anxious. I want this to pass. Please let this pass. I go back to my bed.

I lay for around ten minutes in silence. I get up and go to the white board. I write in big letters:

YOU CAN DO THIS JACK
YOU CAN DO THIS JACK
YOU CAN DO THIS JACK

I sit back down and I stare at the writing. I try to imprint it into my brain. I try to burn the fucker right into my being. I am violently sick again into the bin, I cry, I beg for this to be over, to pass.

Tears roll down my face and I sit in the dark. Repeating to myself the words written shakily on the white board. I cry and I read. I cry and I read. I cry and I read.

Chapter 15: My name is Jack and I'm an alcoholic

Someone knocks on my door. I fell asleep. I get up and I open up the door.

"How we doing, Jack?"

I don't know who this is. A blonde woman with freckles stands in the doorway. She is beautiful.

"Umm, yeah, I've been better," I say. I feel myself going quite red.

"I'm Mel, I'm a support worker here," she says. "Do you mind if we do a breathalyser? I came up earlier and you were out for the count."

"Yeah, of course, sorry," I say.

"Don't apologise! You clearly needed the rest!" she says smiling.

She comes into my room and hands me the breathalyser.

I put it to my lips and I blow into it until I hear the familiar beeps telling me it is finished.

I pass it back to her.

"Okay, it looks like we are all set!" Mel smiles and takes off the tube I blew into and throws it into the bin in my room.

"Would you like to come down and meet some of the residents? They are excited to meet you," Mel says.

"Sure, I am quite nervous though," I say.

"That absolutely natural, Jack, but don't worry you have a lovely group here."

I follow Mel out of the room and we make our way downstairs. I can hear the TV in the front room.

There are two residents sat watching television. One is a frail looking woman in her fifties and another is a young woman with black curly hair.

"Hey, Abbie! Sarah! This is Jack, he has just joined us," Mel says.

The two women look up at me from the sofa. Abbie, the woman with the black curly hair stands up and shakes my hand.

"Hello, mate you all right?" she says.

"Hey, yeah I've been better," I say.

"Don't worry, you will feel good as gold soon," she says.

"All right…" Sarah says, she doesn't take her eyes off the TV.

"Yeah, thanks, you?" I say.

She nods. "What are you in for?" Sarah asks.

"I'm an alcoholic," I say.

"Snap," she says, eyes not leaving the television.

"Don't mind her, she's in a mood because we didn't watch Eastenders," says Abbie, smiling.

"Oh right, I used to watch that a lot," I say.

"Oh fuck me, not another one," Abbie says, smiling.

I laugh.

Mel takes me over to the dining room and a very large man is sitting using a colouring in book.

"This is Brian. He has been with us a few days now. Brian, this is Jack," Mel says.

The large man looks up and beams. He has such an infectious smile I can't help but return it.

"So you're the new guy? The fresh meat!" He says grinning.

I grin back. "Yeah."

"A few things you need to know about me, Jack. I'm fat, I'm fucked up, and I love wearing my wife's clothes," he says, laughing loudly.

I laugh hard. "Well it's very nice to meet you," I say. I already like this guy. Everyone else in the room laughs and I shake his hand. It's a sweaty handshake, the type you would only receive from addicts detoxing, I don't care.

Mel takes me into the garden. It is stunning. There are some chairs and a table in front of me as I walk out. To the right is a beautiful patch filled with flowers. The trees are bare, and the leaves that used to coat them lay in a collage at their feet, littering the ground with a sea of red and brown.

To the far right, I see a couple of residents playing basketball on an old looking court, and to its right are a couple of swings, hanging off an oak frame.

"This is beautiful," I say.

"I thought you might like it out here," Mel says, nudging me with her shoulder.

"Can I smoke?" I say.

"Yeah, of course you can, make sure you use an ashtray though, hang on I'll grab you one." She heads inside and the two residents playing basketball make their way over to me.

"All right, mate? I'm Craig and this is Joe." He holds out his hand and I shake it.

"Hello," I say.

"You just got here a while ago, yeah?" Joe says.

"I did, a few hours ago, I had to be in my room a while until the…"

"…Alcohol leaves your system?" Joe continues.

"Yeah," I say.

"Trust me mate in a couple of days you will feel better. You will be able to eat a shit ton," he says. Joe and Craig smile and laugh.

"Yeah, I haven't eaten in ages. They tried to give me some chicken earlier but I couldn't stomach any of it," I say.

"Yeah, I was the same when I came in," Craig says. "That will pass though, it's all about getting better and eating well."

I nod. "Yeah I can't wait for that."

"Anyway, man, we will catch you in a while," Joe says. They say goodbye and I sit down and roll a cigarette.

Mel comes outside and hands me a black plastic ashtray. "There you go lovely," she says.

"Thank you, I will be back inside in a minute," I say.

"You take your, time Jack, there's no rush." She smiles and walks back inside.

I sit and take in my surroundings.

I don't feel as shit now. I feel a lot better.

The shakes are still here slightly and I feel very weak but I also have started feeling hungry.

For the first time in what feels like forever I can actually feel hunger. No more cider, pretending to fill up my stomach, this is real hunger and I feel ravenous.

I smoke and I sit in the silence. I can hear the birds singing and I can feel the breeze on my face as it moves the trees around me. I smell food. I smell beef. I smell things that set my stomach on fire and make my mouth water. I hear laughing from inside the living room and loud voices talking. I smoke the last of my cigarette and I stub it out into the ashtray.

I get up and walk back into the living room. Craig and Joe are now sitting watching TV as are Sarah and Abbie. Brian still sits colouring at the table.

"Come over here, Jack, let's get to know each other," he says loudly.

I smile and walk over. I pull out a chair and sit opposite him.

"So, how you feeling?" he says, still smiling.

"Yeah, a bit calmer now," I say.

"Yeah, it is very scary when you first arrive. This is my third time here though unfortunately so it doesn't bother me that much meeting new people," he says, looking down at his colouring book. "I've just had a new baby!" he blurts out, grinning.

"Oh really? Congrats," I say.

"Yeah, let's hope she doesn't know I'm not there at the moment. She is only a few weeks old so should be fine." He waves his hand in the air, in a 'not to worry' way.

"So, Jack, how old are you?" he asks.

"Twenty-two," I say.

"*Fuck me*! You're still a baby!" he shouts.

I laugh. "Yeah, I suppose," I say, smiling.

"Do you like card games?" he says.

"Depends what games?" I say.

"You ever play cheat?" he says, grinning.

"I have, I'm pretty good," I say.

"Fuck, yes, cheat it is, my boy!" he shouts, slamming his hand on the table and making me jump. He erupts into laughter and I join him.

"Brian, stop it you made me jump!" shouts Abbie.

"Sorry, babes!" he says loudly. Everyone laughs. I don't at first but it seems they are all used to him and it's okay.

"Can we use that games room whenever we want?" I ask.

"Yes, of course we can, love." Brian says, resuming his colouring. "But we have a meeting there tonight so you may want to check with the prison warden," he says.

I laugh. "Who is that?" I say.

"Tom, the Irish hottie," he says, still colouring in.

"Right, okay," I say laughing.

I get up and walk into the area where the office is. Tom is speaking with someone. They are facing a large whiteboard with all our names on. My name is at the top; next to it is the number of days I will be staying.

"Sorry... Tom?" I say.

He turns around and sees me. "Yes, Jack, you all settled in?" he says.

"Yeah, getting there," I say. "Can I play some pool in that room?"

"Yeah, of course, Jack, you don't need to ask," he responds. "We do have a meeting in there tonight which you are more welcome to come to."

"Yeah maybe," I say. "Can I see how I feel?"

"Yes, absolutely. See you in a while, Jack."

He returns to his conversation and I leave the room and head into the games room. It is cold and the lights are off. I switch them on and walk around the room.

The walls are bare brick and the windows are single paned. It is quite an old building but has been renovated in other areas. I pick up a pool cue and start aimlessly hitting the balls around. I put it down and go over to a wall full of books. I don't really read. I have always wanted to and I really enjoyed English in school. I just didn't pay attention much when I was younger. I didn't care really. I do now.

I sift through the books. Nothing looks familiar.

There is a plasma screen at the far end in the circular area of the room. The chairs are neatly propped against the wall. There is a whiteboard in front of the chairs. I assume this is where they hold meetings and talks.

There are numerous books around the circular area. I spot the *Big Book*. The trusted book of people in AA. I never got on with AA. I don't believe in god, so I don't find it helpful to sit in a room and talk about my 'higher power' when I know it was me that picked up and it can only be me that can stop myself. It works for millions out there though, everyone is different I suppose. Every time I went to a meeting, I didn't like sitting talking about drinking. It made me think about using and I would leave group wanting a drink more than when I walked in.

This doesn't mean I won't try again. I will do anything it takes to aid my recovery. If that means finding a higher power, I might give it a go.

I really want to call my mum. Tell her how things are and see how she is. I know that it's important not to though. She needs the well-deserved rest and I need to stop being so reliant. It hurts but it's the truth.

I exit the room and wander back into the living room. There is a chair free in the corner and I go and sit down. It's very comfortable and I feel exhausted. I curl up and get comfy. I shut my eyes and I listen to everyone talking. I feel calm, slightly withdrawing but I've been worse. It's going to be okay, I feel okay right now. I feel at ease. I don't feel endangered and I don't feel trapped.

I feel myself drifting off and let it happen. Today has been a lot. I feel exhausted.

I am woken by Mel. It is dark outside and I smell food.

"Hey, sleepy head, sorry to wake you but dinner is being served if you would like some?" She is standing over me and I feel groggy.

"Yeah, I guess I should try to eat," I say.

"That's the spirit!" she says.

I get up off the chair and head towards the table. Brian, Craig and Joe are sitting on one side of the table and Abbie and Sarah are on the other next to two residents I haven't met yet. I don't like to sit next to people when I eat but I force myself to on this occasion.

"He has awoken!" Brian says loudly.

I smile and I park myself down on a chair next to him.

"So what's the food like?" I ask.

"Fucking awful. I think they're trying to poison us," Brian says.

Mel taps him on the shoulder. "Don't be mean Brian." She smiles and laughs, I smile nervously.

"No, I'm only kidding, Jack, the grub is pretty gorgeous," he says.

It does look incredible. There is a large amount of beef at the end of the table in a serving station. Vegetables, pasta and an assortment of food sit next to the beef.

"Do we just help ourselves?" I ask Mel.

"Absolutely," she says.

Thank fuck for that. I don't want someone forcing food down my throat if I am not ready to eat, this takes so much of the pressure off me.

I walk over to the trolley of food and size up what I want. I love beef. Can I even eat it though? I guess I won't know until I try.

I put a slice of beef on my plate, a tiny amount of pasta and one carrot.

I head back to the table and I sit down.

"Ah, I remember when I got here, I ate like you, my love," Brian says.

"Oh really?" I say, interested.

"Yup, now look."

I look down at his plate and it is a mountain of gravy, beef, pasta vegetables and potatoes.

"Jesus…" I say.

"Don't be rude, honey," he says. I laugh and he wolfs down a large forkful of beef.

I poke my food and move it around my plate. I don't feel as bad as earlier and my stomach is killing me from hunger.

I load the beef onto my fork and eat. My taste buds wake up and I chew faster and swallow. Fuck me. That was incredible. I eat the rest just as quick.

I then feel a sudden jolt of anxiety. This used to happen every time I ate when I drank. I put my fork down and hold my stomach. Shit, I can't keep this down.

I run to the toilet out of sight of the residents and violently throw up.

I got cocky, I think to myself as I clean up. I look in the mirror and I still look like shit. I hate looking in the mirror, it's like I am expecting to see something else each time, and each time it's the same ghostly face staring back.

"Fuck this," I say to myself.

I head back out and into the dining room. I go back to the food station and put more on my plate. I sit down and eat again. This time it stays down and I eat as much as I can. I feel nervous and anxious but I ignore it. I make sure I eat. I will fucking eat. I have to.

After I finish, I put my plate back on the trolley and I make my way upstairs. Mike has told me I need to take some more medication and also gets some vitamins so I follow him up and wait outside while he gets things set up in the office.

"Okay, mate, in you come," he says, popping his head out of the door.

I walk in and it is just as cold and the light is just as bright. I sit in my chair.

"I'm going to need you up for this one, mate," he says.

I look up confused.

"Why?" I say.

He turns around and is holding a very large needle with yellow, thick liquid inside.

"This is the horrible bit," he says. "I have to give you this injection, in your bum cheek."

Oh fuck. I don't mind injections but that is a big fucking needle.

"Right. Okay. Does it hurt?" I say.

"A little bit, it aches more than hurts," he says, grinning. He starts laughing. I must have a very strange look on my face.

I laugh slightly. "Fuck it, okay, go on then," I say. I stand up and he tells me to pull down my pants on one side of my arse. I do this.

"Okay, Jack, it's going to feel like it's going right into bone, that's what people have said, but don't worry, it isn't. Just stay still and I'll get this done quick."

I brace myself. "Yup, do it," I say.

The needle goes in, deep. Very fucking deep. I have never felt a needle go so deep before. It feels like there is a bone in my arse I never knew about and it's piercing it.

"Oh my fuck," I say, breathing in and out.

"You're doing really well, Jack, one more second," he says, a slight laugh in his voice.

He pulls the needle slowly from my backside, wipes the area clean and puts on a small plaster.

"All done?" I say.

"Yes, well done! You were very calm throughout that," he says, impressed.

"I don't mind needles too much," I say pulling up my pants.

"You will need one of these a day for a few days, I'm afraid. It contains a lot of vitamins and will make you feel a ton healthier," he says.

"I don't care, if it gets me better I'll do a million of them," I say.

"That's it! I won't give you a million though," he says, smiling.

He passes me my tablets and I swallow them.

"These will help your withdrawal."

"Thank you," I say and I drink from a paper cup filled with ice cold water.

"There is a meeting downstairs in an hour if you wanted to go to it. I think it is AA, we have people come in and do talks," he says.

"Hmmm, maybe, I'm still feeling pretty terrible, don't think I can concentrate," I say.

He nods his head. "Yeah that's understandable, mate, it's there if you want it."

"Thanks, Mike"

I get up to leave.

"Can you send Abbie up next?"

I nod. "Sure, thanks again."

"No problem, buddy." He smiles and I leave. Arse hurting as I walk.

I go downstairs into the dimly lit living room. A few of the residents sit on the sofas and chair surrounding the TV.

"You coming to the meeting, love?" Brian says.

"I don't think so, mate," I say back. "Abbie? Mike said can you go up?"

"Cheers, mate," Abbie says. She gets up and heads upstairs.

"I get it, honey, it's your first day and we are all pretty disgusting…" Brian says. He laughs loudly and others do too.

"No, you're not, I'm just pretty tired, still feel pretty shit," I reply.

Brian winks and mouths OK to me. I smile and laugh.

Mel walks in. "Jack would you like some sleep tea?"

"What is that?" I say.

"Oh, it's the best thing about this place!!" Brian says loudly.

"Yeah, Brian has to be one of the only people here who likes it," Mel says, grinning at Brian as he pretends to bow.

"It tastes like shit but it makes you calm as *fuck*!" Brian says. When he says the word 'fuck' his voice breaks and is super high.

I laugh. "Yeah, I'll try it," I say.

"Okay, I will go and brew you some, back in a tick."

Mel walks out of the dining room into the kitchen area which is off limits to residents.

"So, sugar, what do you do on the outside for fun?" Brian asks.

"I used to play music," I say, gazing at the TV. "But I haven't much since I've been fucked up."

I use Brian's word of 'fucked up' to describe what's been going on. It sums it up pretty well.

"Oh, a musician," he says, raising his eyebrows. "Way to go you for not living up to the stereotype!"

We both laugh.

"Yeah, I suppose it is pretty typical. Difference is I am not rich or successful so I have no excuse for going off the rails," I say.

"Oh don't say that, honey, there is still time." He smiles at me.

"So what do you do? When you aren't in here I mean," I ask.

"Fireman," he says.

"No really," I say.

"You cheeky fucker, I'm telling the truth!" he shouts loudly, I can tell he is still joking. "We aren't all fit young men!" He lifts up his arms and flexes his muscles.

"Okay! Sorry, I've never met a fireman before," I say.

"Well, I was one. Until all of this bullshit," he says, flicking his fingers at the rest of the residents. "I drank a lot of red wine. That was my favourite drink, soon turned to spirits and then apparently I was no fun at parties anymore..." He looks down at his hands.

I have a feeling There is a lot more to Brian. I don't pry. I don't know him. I can tell there is a lot of pain behind his eyes. They are kind eyes, but he seems slightly wounded.

I guess I have a while to get to know him anyway.

Mel enters a few minutes later with a mug of 'sleep tea'.

"Good luck." Brian says.

I drink from the mug.

Fuck.

"This tastes of piss," I say.

Mel and Brian burst out laughing, as do most of the other residents.

"Yeah, it tastes bad, but you wait until you sleep. You will be out for the count, lover!" Brian says.

I smile and take another sip. I don't care that it tastes like shit. I want it. I want anything that can help me. I need to sleep and I need to rest. I am exhausted but I am wide awake still.

I sit in the living room and I watch TV with the other residents.

"Okay, group, we have a new resident arriving tomorrow," Tom says as he enters the room and sits on the edge of the sofa nearest the door.

"You won't be the newbie anymore, rockstar," Brian says.

"Please don't call me that," I say smiling.

"Too late, rockstar," he says.

I drink my tea.

"We have a meeting in here in a few minutes, Jack. You don't have to attend as you have just got here but anyone feel free to come in and take your seats." Tom exits the room and walks into the games room.

"You not coming, Hendrix?" Brian says.

"No not tonight, I feel like shit," I say.

"Your loss, baby cakes," he says, and he walks out of the room and goes into the games room with the others.

"I might go to bed," I say to Mel.

"Okay, that's fine, Jack, just make sure you go to the medication room before you head to bed to get your final meds for the night."

"Sure," I say.

I put my mug down and I heave myself off the chair. I walk upstairs. Every single step is an effort. I feel absolutely wiped out. I am starting to shake and sweat pretty badly.

I walk down the corridor and I knock on the medication room door.

"Yup!" says a voice on the other side.

I walk in and a tall man in his early thirties is standing in the room.

"Hello, I'm here for my meds," I say.

"You're Jack, right?" he says. He smiles and he holds out his hand.

"My name is Devansh, But most people here call me Dev." We shake hands.

"Nice to meet you," I say.

I sit down on the same chair as before. Dev looks in the cupboard and pulls out my tablets.

"Here you go, buddy," he says.

"Thank you, man" I say and I chuck the pills into my mouth. I take a swig of the ice cold water and wait. "Do I have to have the injection in my arse again?" I say.

"No, mate," Dev says laughing. "You can look forward to that tomorrow though."

"Ah, fantastic," I say. "Thank you, mate."

"I'm going to be here most the night, Jack, and I will check on you every half hour so leave your door ajar, okay? If you need anything, you just knock"

"I will, thank you, Dev, that means a lot."

I leave the room and go to the toilet. I have a piss and notice it is a dark red colour. This freaks me out a lot. I'd best tell Dev about this at some point. I walk to my room. I am terrified of sleeping. It gives me such bad anxiety. I get scared I will hear things or see things, and I will be alone, in my room, with no one.

I try to push these thoughts out of my head and I climb into my bed. The mattress is hard. I actually prefer this. I have a bad hip so this helps me a lot. I lie down and I shut my eyes.

Thoughts in my head fly in and out. Erratic thoughts of death, withdrawal and seizures. *Stop*, Jack. Fucking relax.

I try and calm my breathing down and I lie still.

I wish I was home.

I wish I wasn't in this fucking bed.

I wish I had my mum here.

I wish I wasn't such a fucking idiot.

I wish I wasn't this way.

I wish I could fucking fall *asleep*.

I open my eyes and look at my white board. I stare at the writing on it.

YOU CAN DO THIS JACK

YOU CAN DO THIS JACK

YOU CAN DO THIS JACK

I can do this. I can do this.

I wake up and I look at the time on the wall.

2.04 a.m.

Most I have slept for a long time.

I am violently shaking in my bed. My clothes and the sheets are soaked through with sweat and I am breathing rapidly.

I need fucking help.

I hear voices coming from the corners of my room. I see silhouettes of figures on my wall. I have to get up.

I get out of my bed and my legs wobble violently. I walk to the medication room and bang on the door.

"Please I need help…" I say.

The door opens and I see Dev standing there.

"Hey, buddy, you okay?" he says.

"I'm withdrawing."

"Yeah, you don't look great, come in and let's get you fixed up."

I enter and I sit on the chair. I am shivering and shaking so much. This is fucking horrible.

"I'm so sorry to do this, I am sorry, man, I really am," I say. I start crying and I can't stop it.

"Hey! Hey, Jack, come on, it is absolutely fine. This is my job, buddy. I am here for you okay? You did a very brave thing coming here yesterday, you're doing great, okay, fella?" he pats me on the back and passes me my pills.

I swallow them fast and drink the water.

"I just feel stupid, I feel so scared," I say, calming down slightly.

"You don't look stupid to me. You look like someone who is trying to get their shit together, which is admirable, Jack." He pats me on the back again.

"Thank you, you're very kind, thank you, really," I say, smiling appreciatively.

"Not a problem, Jack, not a problem."

We sit and talk for a while. I tell him why I am here and how. He tells me not to worry about sleep, and that it is normal to feel the way I do. He gives me a tablet to help me get some rest and I head out of the office into my room.

"Thank you, Dev, you have helped me so much, you have no idea," I say as I leave.

"Not a problem, fella, get some sleep."

I lay back down on my bed and I shut my eyes.

Chapter 16: Group sessions

I am woken by a knock at my door.

"Hi, Jack! Time for medication!"

It's Mel.

"Okay, thank you, I'll get up now."

My bed is soaked in sweat. The important thing is that I slept. I managed to get more sleep last night than I have over the last six months.

I feel weak still. My legs shake slightly as I get out of bed. I pull on my dressing gown, grab my tobacco and I leave my room.

There are only two others out of bed. Craig and Sarah stand by the medical room, not talking. They both look as rough as I feel.

"Morning," I say.

"Morning, mate," Craig says.

Sarah doesn't respond.

I stand behind them and wait my turn. I can hear others being woken by Mel.

"Brian? Knock, knock! It's time for—"

"*Fuck off!*"

He shouts so loudly we all look round.

"Come on, Brian, enough of that, you need to get up and take your meds, I'll leave you to get dressed."

Mel leaves his doorway looking no different from when she knocked. A smile on her face from ear to ear.

"You get used to it!" she says as she passes us.

We all laugh and continue waiting.

I am there for around five minutes before I am invited inside.

I enter and realise it's Mike instead of Dev today.

"Oh hey, Mike," I say.

"Hello, Jack, how did you sleep, mate?"

"Not too bad in the end, started withdrawing in the middle of the night but went to the medical room and Dev helped me out," I say.

"He's golden, isn't he?" Mike says.

"Yeah, he helped me so much, honestly I was so scared last night and I slept great afterwards."

"Jack, that's brilliant. Now, I have to give you this wonderful injection again. Are you ready?" he looks at me hesitantly.

"Oh fuck, I forgot about that. Yeah, okay, go ahead I'm ready."

I stand up, pull down my pants on one side and brace once more.

The injection is deep and painful. I don't care. It's good for me and I know it is.

"Well done, mate, all done," Mike says.

I pull up my pants and sit back down, as best I can.

"That stuff does you a ton of good though, you will notice the affect soon," he says,

"I hope so," I say.

Mike passes me some Librium and Vitamin B tablets. I scoff them down.

"That's you done, bud," Mike says.

I stand up and shake his hand. "Pleasure doing business with you," I say,

He laughs as I leave.

I head downstairs and don't hear anyone else. I walk through the living room and head out the doors leading to the garden.

I sit down and I roll myself a cigarette. It is very cold today.

I spark up my cigarette and shut my eyes. I have survived my first night. My first night ever, without any alcohol, I did it.

I feel so proud. My mum would be proud. I miss her. I can speak to her tomorrow though.

I am still scared and homesick. That hasn't left me yet. I feel anxious here and I want that feeling to go.

Brian comes out of the doors. "Morning, love," he says. His hair is spiked up and his face is red and puffy.

"Sorry for the commotion this morning, I was half naked when the officer barged in."

I laugh. "Morning, Brian," I say.

"How do you feel today?" he says. He sits on the bench next to me and sparks up his cigarette.

"Very shit," I say. "I miss my family."

He looks at me thoughtfully. "Me too, Hendrix, me too."

I smile and laugh.

"It never gets easy being away from your family, Jack, but you have to remember why you are doing this, you're doing it for them," Brian says, his voice serious.

"Yes, exactly, I have to keep reminding myself that," I say.

I stand up. It's too cold. "I'm going to make a coffee," I say. "You want one?"

"Ooh you read my mind, yes please, love, two sugars!"

I walk towards the doors and let myself in. He's a bit much in the morning. I need quiet and peacefulness right now.

I head into the residents' kitchen. It's very small, has a fridge, a sink and a kettle. There is a window that looks out onto the car park. I switch on the kettle and gaze out of the window.

I wonder what my family is doing now. I think about people I haven't thought about in a long time. Ex-girlfriends,, people from school and so on. I wonder what they are doing now.

They sure as shit aren't looking out a window at a detox facility. I sigh and I start making the coffee. I like mine black, no sugar.

I used to have sugar but I don't feel I need it just now. I drink the coffee and feel the burn in my stomach and it feels good.

I walk into the dining room and place Brian's coffee on the table. I knock on the window and gesture to him that it's on the table. He blows a kiss. I laugh.

I sit down on the sofa and switch on the TV. I don't really want to watch anything, I just need some noise in the room.

Joe and Craig have come downstairs chatting.

"How you feeling, Jack?" Craig says.

"Getting there, mate," I say.

He smiles and he and Joe head to the kitchen. Tom comes into the room with Lynne and they get everyone's attention. By this time everyone is pottering about downstairs.

"Okay, everybody, we will have a talk happening with myself in the games room later, I would like you all to be there please. Also has the house leader put up your jobs for the week? If so please make sure you complete those in your free time." Tom finishes talking and spots me.

"Jack, how are we doing today?"

"Better than yesterday but still pretty rough."

"Rome wasn't built in a day, lad, give it time." He smiles and continues addressing the group. "Also as I mentioned yesterday we have a new resident arriving today, please make sure to be as welcoming as you were to Jack here." He pats me on the shoulder and everyone nods.

Tom walks off with Lynne and we all go back to our morning.

Brian goes over to the table and starts colouring in again. I guess it relaxes him. "Thank you for the coffee,

Hendrix," he shouts in a monotone voice that makes me laugh.

"Sure," I say.

I head back upstairs and I start unpacking my bag.

Yesterday feels like a long nightmare. I created this idea of what detox would be like and when I arrived it was a shock.

Not necessarily a bad shock but when something isn't what you expect it throws you. Well it does for me.

I sit on my head and read my white board. I say it back to myself again.

YOU CAN DO THIS JACK.

I stand up and I place a tick on the board. Part of me thinks this is counting down the days. Part of me thinks I am agreeing with the writing.

I lie back on my bed and shut my eyes. I could sleep again. I can't though. I know I have to be in this group today. I get out my notebook and I start writing about what has happened since I got here. Who I've met, what I've experienced and what it's like.

I want to one day look back on this. I want to learn from it. I want it to be so fresh in my mind that this never happens again.

I get up, grab my shower gel and head out of my room.

The corridor is empty.

I head to the shower room and walk in.

An old woman is sitting on the toilet completely naked.

"Oh fuck, I am so sorry!" I turn and shut the door as fast as I can.

"Why didn't you knock?!" says the voice from inside.

I want to tell her to lock the fucking door. I mean that's pretty standard. I don't say this though. I am very embarrassed.

"Honestly I just didn't think, I am very sorry."

Good start Jack. Fuck sake.

I go back to my room and wait until I hear the woman leave the shower room. I get up and head to the door. I knock. I enter.

I knew I hadn't met all of the residents yet but that was slightly trial by fire. 'Good to meet you I've seen your breasts'. I want to crawl in a hole and die. Or sleep.

I lock the door, strip down and get into the shower. The water is cold. I try my best to fix it, nothing works.

I just stay inside and bear it. I stand in the cold water and rest my head against the wall.

Fuck me. Good start to the day.

I get out and dry myself off. I wrap the towel around my bottom half and leave. There is a queue outside.

"Oh fuck." For some reason I hold my hands over my chest. I don't know why I do this but it makes a lot of them laugh.

"Show us your tits, Jack," I hear Brian say.

I stick up my middle finger and hurry to my room. Why did I grab my tits? Fuck it; I've done a lot more embarrassing things than that.

I put on some clean and warm lounge clothes. I look in the mirror and still can't stand the sight of myself.

Disgusting.

Pale.

Ugly.

Alcoholic.

I stay in my room for a while and stare out of my window. It looks like it's going to snow. I hear a knock on my door.

"Yeah?" I say.

The door opens slightly.

"Hendrix, come on, I was only kidding!"

It's Brian. I laugh.

"Don't be silly, man, I know you were I'm just chilling."

"Okay, rockstar, well, come down in a minute as we have group, and put on a bra," he says. He says the last bit fast and comically and it makes me laugh hard.

I put my clothes away in my cupboard and I head downstairs. As I get to the bottom of the stairs, I see the old woman from the toilet.

"Again, I am really sorry," I say.

She smiles at me, apparently not embarrassed at all. "Accidents happen, what's your name?"

"Jack," I say.

"Mine's Pat."

I hold out my hand and we shake.

"Okay great, I still feel terrible though."

"Stop! It's fine, we have group, let's go in."

We walk into the games room and I see the chairs are off the wall they were propped against and made into a circle.

Tom stands at the whiteboard and ushers us in.

"Okay, everyone, sit down wherever you like and we can get started."

I sit down. Brian sits to my right and Abbie sits to my left.

"Okay, today we are talking about how our addiction began to control our lives and how we acted when we were in active addiction," Tom says.

You can tell he has done this a million times, I don't care though. He is easy to listen to and very direct.

Tom draws a bubble on the white board and in the middle writes MY ADDICTION.

"Okay, so what I want you to do is come up here and write something you lost because of your addiction. This can be anything. It can be the loss of control, family, friends or a job."

I think for a minute. I mean, really, I lost all of these things because of my addiction.

I raise my hand.

"Jack, yes, show us what you got," Tom says.

I stand up and approach the board. I draw a line coming off the bubble and write BODILY FUNCTIONS.

"Ah, okay, Jack! This is a common one for addicts. As you begin to use and not take care of yourself your body starts to deteriorate over time. So yes, a good start."

I sit back down. Others raise their hands and approach the board listing off a number of things:

Job

Motivation

Relationships

Self-worth

Respect

And so on.

"Brian, you haven't raised your hand. Anything you want to put on the board?" Tom says.

Brian looks up from the ground and I realise he looks upset. His eyes are red and he looks sad. "No," HE says. He looks back down at the ground and Tom looks at him.

"You know at some point you will have to share, Brian," he says.

"I'm good, thanks," Brian responds.

I don't know why but it becomes very tense all of a sudden. Tom moves on. Brian keeps his eyes to the floor and doesn't seem to want to engage in the group. I nudge him and mouth 'Are you okay?' He looks at me and nods. Then continues looking at the floor.

I listen and participate in the rest of the group. We talk about ways we acted in our addiction. Violence, anger, sadness and despair.

"I have done a lot I'm not proud of," I say.

Others in the room nod and agree.

"It's about recognizing that, Jack, but also about learning from it and ultimately forgiving yourself for things you did in active addiction," Tom says.

"I hurt so many people," I say. "I never wanted to hurt anyone. When I was using all I was thinking about is where the next drink is coming from. I would have a ton of alcohol in the house and still be worried about when it runs out. It was a constant stress."

"Yup, me too," Craig says.

Everyone nods in agreement.

The rest of the group potters on and we eventually leave and head out for a cigarette.

"Well done on talking in your first group, Jack," Joe says.

"Oh right, yeah, thanks," I say. "I thought I had to?"

"No, not at all, you saw Brian, he hasn't said a thing in any group since he has arrived."

"Yeah, why is that?" I say.

"I'm not sure." Joe says. "Tom knows, as he knows Brian quite well, but we have no idea."

I nod and shrug.

"I guess we'll see," I say.

I sit and I listen to the others talk about group. It was okay, I guess. It is stuff that I already knew I lost so I think it wasn't as hard hitting.

"Where is Brian?" I ask Pat.

"I think he is still in with Tom," she says.

I look through the window of the games room and see them sitting down opposite each other. Brian looks like he is crying.

I realise I shouldn't be looking at this and I head back inside.

I go back up to my room and I sit on my bed and pull out my journal. I write about the day and I look at my whiteboard.

I let the words sink in some more.

I start feeling anxious and my hands start shaking.

I head to the medical room and knock on the door. Mike answers.

"All right, Jack?" he says.

"Yeah, I'm feeling pretty rough again," I say.

"Hold out your hands for me, mate."

I lift my hands into the air and they shake violently.

"Yeah, you're shaking quite a lot, sit down and let's sort you out," he says.

I sit down and stare out of the window.

"What was this place before it was a detox centre?" I ask.

"Someone's home," he replies, his back to me, getting my medication ready.

"Wow, it does feel like that here."

"Yeah, it's been a detox centre for a while now but it does have a cosy feeling to it." He turns around and hands me some Librium and vitamins.

I chuck them in my mouth and swallow.

"Thanks, Mike," I say.

"No problem, mate."

I get up and I leave. Brian is standing directly outside the door.

"Hey, man, you okay?" I say.

"Yup," he replies.

"Okay. I'm going to head downstairs, see you in a bit?" I say.

"Yup."

Chapter 17: New Arrival

I walk off and head downstairs.

I hear people in the reception area. There is an ambulance outside and a man getting out with someone carrying his bags.

He looks in a bad way.

His clothes are torn and his face is bright red and bloated. He his met by Lynne and she helps him into the reception.

I'm assuming this is the new guy.

I walk into the living room and sit down. The Librium has started to kick in and I feel very calm.

Abbie joins me on the sofa.

"Where you from, Jack?" she asks.

"Tunbridge Wells, born in Hammersmith," I say.

I don't know why I always say where I was born. It's become sort of a tic.

"Oh nice! I'm from Chatham," she says.

"That's near here isn't it?" I say.

"Yeah, sort of, I was living in Hoxton for a while, sleeping rough."

"Fuck, really?" I say.

"Yeah, someone called an ambulance for me because I was having a seizure on the side of the road," she says.

"Jesus," I say, "there is so much about alcohol withdrawal I wish I knew before."

"I know right! I've come off crack and heroin before and never been as scared as I was this time," she says.

I never tried anything like that. I'm glad I haven't. Knowing my personality I don't think it would end well at all.

Abbie is very pretty. You can tell she has had it tough. She has a scar on her forehead which she tells me was from a knife. She was having sex with someone for money to feed her crack addiction and the guy wouldn't pay, so they fought and he pulled a knife.

Apparently he is in prison now. I don't know whether I believe a lot of what I hear in here about people's stories. I guess I have never heard such stories before and they shock me. Which doesn't mean to say they aren't true, I have just haven't ever known people who have lived such horrors.

"You fancy a coffee?" I say.

"Yes please," she says.

I get up and head to the kitchen and make a coffee for us both. I exit and see Brian sitting on a chair near to us watching TV. He looks in a better mood.

"Sorry, mate, I would've made you a drink if I knew you were here," I say, putting my and Abbie's coffee on the table next to us.

"Don't worry yourself love," he says, smiling and turning back to the TV.

"Brian says you're a musician?" Abbie says.

"Yeah, well, I try to be," I say.

"What type of music do you do? I like house and drum and bass," she says.

"You won't like my music then!" I say, laughing.

"No! I like all sorts!" she says, smiling.

"I write acoustic stuff really, quite bluesy music."

"That's cool, how long for?" she says.

"Since I was about fifteen," I say.

"Ohh, nice!"

It's nice that they actually want to know about me. Everyone I know knows everything about me so it's refreshing to have new people interested.

"So did you come from the hospital to here?" I ask Abbie.

"Yeah, mate," she says. "Was in a bad way. Was sent here as soon as I was able."

"Oh right, I came from home," I say.

"You have your own place?" Brian asks.

"No, I live with my mum at the moment," I say. "She's basically been my carer whilst I've been drinking."

"Poor fucking woman," Brian says.

"Yup. I miss her. She needs this time away from me though, I've been making her life a living hell," I say, ashamed.

Abbie and Brian nod. I stop talking and we watch TV.

Tom enters the room.

"Right everyone, Paul is here and he is going to be staying in his room a while until later."

"Is he the new guy? I think I saw him outside," I say.

"That's the one," Tom says.

"What is he like?" Abbie asks.

"You can see for yourself when he comes down," Tom says. He exits the room and heads upstairs. We see the new guy Paul follow behind Tom.

"Fuck, he looks worse than you, Jack." Brian says.

"It's not a competition, Brian," I say smiling.

"If it was he would win, poor love," he says, watching Paul round the corner of the stairs.

"I think he came from hospital, there was an ambulance outside," I say.

"Yeah, most likely." Abbie says.

Mel comes into the front room. She is wearing a matching red top and joggers, I always find myself blushing when she is around.

"How we doing, everyone? Lunch in five," she says. "You settling in okay, Jack?" I go red.

"Yeah! Yes, thank you, everyone has been very lovely," I say.

"I hear you met Pat yesterday," she says smiling and raising her eyebrows.

"Oh, Jesus, don't," I say, going redder and putting my face in my hands.

"Don't worry about it, Jack, she found it funny," she says laughing.

"I'm glad someone did!" I say, also laughing.

I hear a door opening in the dining room and the cook appears with a trolley.

There is meatloaf, pizza and salad.

I am starving. I get up off the sofa and make my way over to the dining area. I pick up a plate and I stand over the food, looking at the wide selection.

I feel starving hungry today. I feel like I can eat.

I don't put a lot on my plate. I get some meatloaf, one slice of pizza and some salad. I figure the salad will be easier to digest but the meatloaf and pizza will be a struggle.

I sit down in the nearest chair and I pick up my knife and fork.

I have never had meatloaf before. I hear about it a lot in films, Americans seem to love it. I put some on my fork and eat.

It tastes amazing. Like a burger really. There are onions and herbs I can't pin inside it. I shut my eyes and I chew. I don't feel anxious eating today. I think the Librium I just had is probably helping a lot.

I finish off the meatloaf, eat some pizza and tuck into the salad.

"Looks like your appetite is back, Hendrix," Brian says raising his eyebrows at me.

"Don't speak too soon, man, we will see," I say.

The tough bit comes after I have eaten. Whether or not it will stay down is yet to be seen. I feel okay. My anxiety has spiked again but I ride it out.

I can feel my heart in my throat and I feel wiped out. My body is most likely still working it's hardest to try and digest the food I eat.

I leave the table, take my plate over to the trolley and go and sit down on the sofa. I watch TV and I try to not focus on the food I just ate. I am not going to get better if I don't keep my food down.

I feel bad for leaving the table whilst people are still eating but I need space after I eat. The anxiety makes it beyond difficult to talk to people and I can't focus on anything apart from what is going on in my head.

I start sweating. I start shaking. Fuck.

I have to get past this. I will be okay. This will pass.

Brian finishes eating and joins me on the sofa.

"Feel sick?" he says.

"Yup. Sorry, man, I need to be quiet for a bit," I say.

"Don't worry, love, I know the feeling," he says.

He starts rolling a cigarette and offers me one. I accept.

We both get up and head outside. We spark up a cigarette.

"Sorry about earlier, Jack," Brian says.

"That's okay, I didn't want to pry and ask what was up," I say.

"It's complicated," he says. "There are things I need to address and Tom wants me to talk about it and I find it difficult."

"I get it, mate," I say.

I do. It's hard to talk about things that hurt. Especially in front of a room full of people.

I have a feeling I will have to share soon. I am not looking forward to it.

"I'm not really a firefighter," he says.

"Yeah, I guessed that..." I say smiling.

He laughs too and we sit there in silence for a while, smoking.

"Come on, love, let's go back in." Brian gets up.

"Yeah, okay." I get up too and follow him inside.

Most people have finished eating now and are all lounging in the front room. I join them and sit down on the sofa. Abbie looks round and makes a strange face. I follow her eyes and I look round.

Paul, the new guy, is walking down the stairs with his bags and his jacket on. He isn't wearing any trousers. He still looks red and bloated.

I nudge Brian and he looks over. "What the fuck," he says.

"Hey, are you Paul? I'm Abbie, are you okay?" she says, getting up and going to the door of the front room.

Paul responds but no one can really hear what he is saying.

"Sorry, babe, what did you say? Shall I get someone for you?" Abbie says, getting closer to him and steadying him as he wobbles on the spot.

"I'm just popping to the shop," Paul says. His eyes won't focus and he is trying to get past Abbie.

"No, mate, you're in detox and you have just got here, you can't just yet," Abbie says.

"I always get beers from the shop when I'm here. I've been waiting for this holiday. Tell Mum I'll be back in a bit," Paul says. It's at this moment I realise Paul is hallucinating and not in a good way. I start to panic. I get up fast and walk past Paul and Abbie. I head to the office.

"Tom, Paul is downstairs and he is withdrawing, he thinks he is somewhere else. He's hallucinating."

Tom immediately puts down his cup of tea and follows me out. He approaches Paul.

"Paul? *Paul!* Do you know where you are?" Tom says loudly to Paul.

"Eastbourne!" Paul says.

"No, Paul, you are in detox in Maidstone. Do you want to come upstairs and get some rest?" Tom says.

Paul is trying to get past and looks completely lost. "Okay…" he says.

"Come with me, Paul," Tom says holding his arm and turning him around to lead him upstairs. Lynne approaches Tom behind him. Tom turns to her.

"Call an ambulance, Lynne," Tom says calmly.

"Okay, is he okay?" Lynne says.

"He's in DTs, we need to get the ambulance now," Tom says.

Lynne turns and jogs into the office. Tom leads Paul upstairs slowly.

"Fuck," I say.

My heart is thumping in my head. I feel dizzy and anxious. It's one thing to experience delirium tremens, but to see someone else hallucinating is terrifying. I know the confusion and how scary it is. I feel so sad and very emotional. I don't want anyone to go through that. He has no family with him and is alone. I feel awful.

Now I see what my mum was dealing with. This is genuinely terrifying. I get up and I head into a room next to the dining room that is meant for chill out time.

I sit and put my head in my hands. The sweat falls off my forehead. I need to calm down. This has brought this back in my mind I wasn't ready for. I can't breathe.

I am trying to get air into my lungs and nothing is happening. My chest tightens and I feel adrenaline surging through my veins. My heart. My fucking heart is going to explode. I open my eyes and everything is blurred. I see flecks of light that look like stars. I black out.

I am woken by Tom. He stands over me and is saying my name.

"I think I blacked out," I say.

"What happened?" he asks.

"I thought I was having a heart attack," I say, clutching my chest and breathing slowly.

"Oh right. You had a panic attack. Don't worry I understand you seeing that will have brought up a lot for you. How are you feeling now?" he says, sitting on the edge of the sofa.

"I feel okay, I feel shaky."

"Get yourself up stairs and see Mike, it's time for your meds," he says, patting my back.

I stand up and walk out of the room.

Brian stands by the door as I leave.

"I came in and you were out of it!" he says.

"I had a panic attack, I'm okay now though…" I say.

I pass him and head towards the stairs.

I walk up and go to the medical room.

I go inside and tell Mike what happened.

"Yeah, Paul has been taken to hospital. We can deal with withdrawals here but he was in a bad way," he says.

I am glad he has gone to hospital. I would've hated it if he stayed here, not because I didn't want him to, but because I would be worried about him.

I take my Librium and I head to my room. I sit down and put my head down onto my pillow. I shut my eyes and try to think of something else. Anything else. Images of what I went through in hospital flash in my mind and make me panic. I try my hardest to focus on the white board and what I wrote on it. I can do this. Breathe. Just breathe.

I shut my eyes.

I'm in a bright room. The ball of mass from before floats in the middle of the room. It grinds and hums as it spasms, getting larger and more aggressive. It shrinks down and stays minuscule for a moment. I reach out, I want to touch it, and I want to control it. It explodes with a deafening screech, bright white blinds me.

I wake up.

That same fucking dream. I don't know what it means but I always remember it so clearly. The fear. The feeling of danger and uncertainty. The terror when it explodes. I hate that fucking dream.

I head back downstairs and realise everyone is in group. I didn't mean to miss it, I'm sure they will understand. I sit down and Lynne enters.

"No group, Jack?" she says looking sceptical.

"I fell asleep. Will I be in trouble?" I say.

"No, they will understand. If you like, when they all come out I am doing guided medication, would you like to try it?"

This isn't something I have ever done before. I hate being in a quiet space with just my thoughts and usually avoid it at all costs. Maybe this will help with my recovery. Maybe it will help me sleep.

"Yeah, sure. Is it like hypnosis?" I say.

Lynne laughs. "You could say that. No, it's more for relaxation and if you suffer with anxiety this will help a lot."

"I do suffer from it, very much. I will do it," I say.

"Great, follow the others when they come up, okay?" she says.

"I will, thanks, Lynne."

She walks off up the stairs and I sit in the silent living room waiting for the others to get out of group.

I hear the door go and people file out into the living room.

"You coming to meditation?" Brian asks.

"I am, what's it like?" I say.

"Fucking gorgeous," he says.

I laugh.

I follow Brian, Pat, Abbie and Sarah upstairs. We turn right on the landing and enter a room located above the games room. We walk in and I see there are six bean bags on the floor, the lights are off and he curtains are drawn. About our heads, the oast roof interior is littered with fairy lights and it extends high above our heads.

I slump myself down on the beanbag closest to me.

Lynne has her back to us. She is trying to work the CD player.

She turns to us all and exhales.

"Okay! So! Welcome to guided meditation! Today Jack is joining us for the first time, Jack, welcome," she says.

everyone looks at me and I nod my head.

"Thanks for having me," I say.

Lynne asks us all to lie back on our beanbags and she walks around handing us small purple sacks that smell strongly of lavender.

"Okay, now close your eyes and place the sack across them," she says. I notice that her voice has changed to a relaxed tone.

I put the sack over my eyes.

Lynne presses play on the CD player and the sound of electronic relaxing keys starts playing.

Lynne begins to tell us that we are in a forest. The forest is deep and dark, and we are right in the heart of it.

"You walk along a dirt path and you find a pool of water."

I can't concentrate. I'm trying my hardest to imagine this pool of water in the forest but I can't focus. My anxiety is bad right now.

I need to relax.

I breathe. I try with all my strength to picture the pool of water.

"You enter the pool, the water feels nice against your skin," Lynne continues.

I can see it, I can feel it. I am starting to feel relaxed.

I picture myself healthy. I picture myself looking better than I have ever felt. I am sitting in the water and the sun is warm, beating down on my head.

A flash ignites my vision. I open my eyes and look around. Everyone still has their eyes shut. I shut my eyes again and try to picture the pool. Nothing. Just white, that white room, with that black mass floating in the middle. I open my eyes.

I don't want this. I don't want to be in here. I don't know why I thought this was a good idea. I get up off of the beanbag.

"Are you okay, Jack?" Lynne says.

"Sorry… I need some air," I say.

I get out of that room as fast as I can. I don't know why I keep seeing the same thing every time I try to calm down or relax. I don't know what it means and it fucking scares me.

I go downstairs and exit into the garden. I roll a cigarette. My hands are shaking and I feel sick. I smoke it fast. Mike enters the garden.

"Jack? I thought you were in meditation?" he says, sitting down next to me.

"I was. I keep getting this horrible vivid dream every time I start to relax or drift off," I say. "It's starting to scare me and it's terrifying. I don't know what to do."

I feel myself getting worked up and feel tears coming. I stop them.

"Have you seen Angie yet?" Mike says.

"No. Who's that?" I say.

"She is a psychiatrist; she is here twice a week. I will speak to Tom and get an appointment set up with her for you."

I look at Mike.

"Will that actually help me though?" I ask. "I've been seen my psychiatrists my entire life, no one has been able to tell me anything new."

"Well maybe she can help you in this part of your recovery. Help you understand what is happening to your mental state whilst you are going through this," he says.

"Yeah, okay. Thanks, Mike." I get up and walk back inside.

I get to call my mum tomorrow. I am really looking forward to it but I am also scared. I want to scream down the phone to come and get me. I can't do that. To her or myself.

I don't feel happy today. I feel fucking shit. I want to feel normal and not feel this way.

I tell Mike I am going to bed. I head upstairs and don't respond when people say hello. I am going to get into bed and sleep. That's all I want.

I want this day to end.

I want to be normal.

Chapter 18: Forgiveness

"There are six other people you can be asking questions to, Tom."

"Yes, but I am asking you, Brian."

"I don't know what you want me to say. I don't want to talk about it"

"Tough shit, Brian. Do you think Abbie wanted to talk about it? Or Joe? Or Craig? No. They spoke because they know they have to, for their own good."

"Yes well, I am not them, Tom. Get off my fucking back."

Brian gets up and kicks the chair he was sitting in across the floor.

"Stay in the room, Brian. Stay with it. Tell us why you're angry. Tell us what's making you upset."

"*You* are!" Brian shouts. This makes me jump. "I know the stuff I did was wrong. I don't want to talk about it in front of all of these people!"

"So you are ashamed, is that it?" Tom says, pressing on.

"Of course I am fucking ashamed!" Brian shouts back.

Brian stands in the corner of the room rubbing his face in his hands and paces to and from the door.

"I've done things I am ashamed of, Brian," I say. "I have hurt people I love, I have broken bridges with people I cared about."

"Hang on a sec, Jack," Tom says holding his hand up. "I appreciate you're trying to make Brian feel better, but he needs this."

I shut my mouth.

"So you were telling us you were fired from your job, Brian," Tom continues. "And then what?"

Brian stays silent and breathes in and out deeply in the corner of the room.

He walks back over to the circle of chairs and picks up the one he launched across the room. He sits down, head in his hands.

"I went home and got drunk…" he says.

"Did your wife know you were drinking again?"

"No," Brian says, wiping his eyes.

"And then what."

"I got angry. I don't know why. It wasn't at Jane. She was asleep," Brian says staring out the window with tears in his eyes.

"Okay and then what happened?" Tom says.

"I didn't know what to do. All I kept thinking about was how useless I was."

Everyone is silent now.

"I took a knife and I slit my wrists," he says, fast and very matter of fact.

"Okay," Tom says.

"I took an overdose of sleeping pills and I sat in the bath."

Brian starts to cry. It breaks my heart. To see such a large, friendly man, break.

"It's okay." Abbie says patting his back.

"My wife found me. I don't remember when. It can't have been long after," he says. "She called an ambulance and I was taken to hospital."

"Thank you for sharing that with us, Brian," Tom says. "You know why I had to press you to share, don't you?"

Brian nods and cries into his hands. "I am here for her, and for my baby," he says, wiping his eyes and sitting up. "Jane saved my life and has been amazing. I need to do this and be better for her and the baby."

I smile and nod.

"You also need to forgive yourself, Brian. You know what you did was fucking stupid. You weren't yourself and luckily nothing too life changing happened, *this* time. You need to accept it and move on from it stronger and more determined to stay clean. Otherwise it isn't just you in danger, it is your family too," Tom says.

Brian nods and smiles at Tom.

Tom continues the group and we discuss guilt and shame. Brian is a lot more open now and is talking to Tom and us about what happened and how he feels about it.

Guilt and shame is something I have a fair amount of experience in. In the early days of me cutting down I would hide drink wherever I could. Behind the fridge, under the sofa, outside in a bush, anywhere. I learned to be more and more deceitful and used my skills at lying on a daily basis. My whole life ended up being too much. The lies pile on top of one another and everything gets out of hand.

The shame would be there in great amounts. Drinking in public at times I shouldn't, arguments with my mum in public when I am drunk and worst of all, losing control of my bodily functions so I can't even leave the house without shitting myself. It gets to a point where it all feels too much.

The thing that a lot of people don't understand is when, inside your head, your daily life is a nightmare, a struggle and you can't take it, you feel more alone than anyone on Earth. I have sat in a room full of people before and felt nothing but loneliness and sadness that I couldn't make go away. Until I drank. Drink, for me, would solve that problem. It would numb the pain and make me forget. Or so I thought.

It, in fact, does the opposite of that. It all builds up. You become reliant on the numb feeling. Your body adapts itself to the amount you ingest. So when you want to stop, your body won't let you, because you are dependant.

"What I want to know is why drink doesn't come with a warning label like cigarettes," I say.

Everyone in the room looks around.

"Would that have made you not drink, though, Jack?" Tom asks.

"I don't know. I honestly don't know. If I had known that it isn't like cigarettes, that when your body is dependent on alcohol and you decide to stop, that can almost die, yeah, maybe I wouldn't have treated it carelessly and treated it more like a class A drug," I say.

A lot of the residents nod their heads.

"The problem is that I was never taught about withdrawal. I wasn't taught about the dangers of alcohol. I was only ever told 'You can get addicted'. Well that doesn't tell me shit. That is a broad thing to say for such a specific, dangerous substance. This shit can kill you if you get dependant. Your body can shut down if you *don't* drink after a certain point," I say, feeling myself getting angry. "If you had told me that, yeah, Tom, I may have had second thoughts about picking up."

"I notice you're getting angry."

"Yeah, I am pissed off that I am in here when every other fucker out there is able to be normal and isn't affected by it. I am angry that a liquid is able to control me in ways that have destroyed everything I love. Of course I am angry!" I respond.

Tom nods his head as do a few others.

"And that is normal, Jack. The fact that you have become addicted to alcohol doesn't make you sub normal. Addiction affects millions upon millions, and it is about learning to live without that substance in your life controlling you," he says.

"Right. So I am twenty-two. I have to live another possible fifty years without ever being able to take someone out for a drink? Without going to parties? Without being normal? Is that what you're telling me?"

"What do you think, Jack?" Tom says.

"Yeah, okay..." I say. I feel upset and shit. I do want to stop, but the gravity of what this addiction has done to the rest of my life has just settled in. Never? I can't drink *ever* again.

Fuck.

"Can I call my mum, please?" I say.

"Yes of course, can you do it after group?"

"No, I want to talk to her now."

"Okay, Jack, that's fine."

Everyone is silent as I get up and leave group. I am furious. I am upset. I want to crawl into a hole and fucking die. *Forever*! I am supposed to stop drinking forever. Why the fuck did I have to get this way. Why the fuck am I not normal.

I go to the phone in the hallway next to the TV room. I pick it up. I dial the number and I listen to it ring.

"Hello?"

"Mum?"

"Jack! Hey, darling, how are you doing? How is it?"

"Mum, I am scared…" I break down. I cry down the phone.

"Oh, Jacko, I know, I know it's difficult. You are doing so well, love. I know it's scary but look how far you have come. What are the people like there?" she says, trying to calm me down.

"I am scared. I am so sad I have fucked things up this much. I can never drink again and I am devastated," I reply crying into the phone.

"Jacko. Last week, you were hallucinating, more terrified than I have ever seen you. You never ate, you couldn't control your body functions, and you weren't living, love. You are lucky to be alive! Why would you be upset about never drinking again after what it has done to you?" she says.

She's right. I know she is fucking right. Even now, when I am getting better, I am still trying to defend drink. Still clawing at a possibility of drinking again after it almost killed me. I feel fucking pathetic.

"I know. I know you're right. I am just scared my friends won't want to be around me sober. That I won't be myself anymore…" I say, calming my breathing.

"If your friends don't want to see you sober, they aren't friends, are they," my mum says.

I stay silent a moment and I think. "Yeah. You're right. I am sorry. I am sorry to call you like this. Today has been hard. I am getting better though and I am eating finally," I say.

"Jacko, that is amazing! We are all so proud of you love. Everyone is asking after you and send their love. I will come and see you tomorrow, anyway, just stay strong and remember how proud we all are."

"I will, thank you, Mum, I really needed to hear that. I'll see you tomorrow. Love you."

"Okay, love, love you too! See you soon!" she says.

I put down the phone and I shut my eyes and breathe. I needed to hear that. It's crazy how easily your mind can trick you into missing something you thought you loved, even if it tried to kill you. Drink is not my friend. It hates me. I need to learn to hate it, not love it. I can't live that way anymore. My mum is right. I have to be stronger.

I have to make this count and get better.

I go back into the room and I apologise to Tom.

"I am sorry for getting angry and leaving," I say.

"Don't apologise, Jack, it's okay."

"No, I feel stupid I am sorry."

Tom smiles and nods.

"That was just a bit of a shock to realise I could never drink again. I kind of knew that deep down, but it was still a shock," I say.

"Of course, Jack, it is a huge thing to deal with, but that is why you're here. It's why all of you are here," he says, looking at everyone.

I smile.

Our group ends and we all leave the games room.

I feel sick. Out of nowhere the withdrawal starts up again. By now I have still been vomiting a few times throughout the days I've been here, so I know what to expect. I head to the toilet. Slump myself down by the toilet and throw up. I get up, wash my face and go up to the medical room.

I knock and enter. Mike gives me my Librium and vitamins and I leave.

I don't mind being sick anymore. It is part of my day and I feel used to it.

"Where is Dev?" I ask Tom downstairs.

"He is mainly on night shifts, he is in tomorrow evening though, you two get on?"

"Yeah, he's all right," I say.

I head into the living room and go over to the dining area. We have jacket potatoes today. I still don't feel a hundred percent. It varies really. I cut a potato in half and eat it with some salad.

It's good.

Brian is having an argument with Mel.

"Jack called his mum today, why can't I call my wife?"

"Brian, you can call her tonight, you already spoke to her this morning."

"I don't care, I miss her and want to speak to her!"

"Speak to Tom, Brian, but he will most likely say the same as me."

Brian gets up and slams his plate on the table. He walks off into the office and I see Tom shut the door.

"Is he okay?" I ask Abbie.

She swallows her food and speaks. "He is very up and down, he's a great bloke but just is a bit all over the place."

"Fair enough," I say.

I can understand that. Every day for me feels that way. I can feel great and settled in the morning and by lunch I can feel like I want to end it all. I have never found out why this is. For a while I thought everyone felt normal and I was mad. When you come somewhere like this where people are like me, it reminds you that you aren't mad, you are just struggling like so many others.

I get up and put my plate in the trolley.

"What are my jobs?" I ask Mel.

"Oooh, I am not sure, Jack, the board is over there by the stairs."

I walk over and I look on the board. Dotted around it are letters from ex residents, some famous, saying thank you and how this place saved their life.

I move across the board and I find the sheet of paper with jobs. It reads:

Craig: toilet (entrance)
Abbie: bathroom (upstairs)
Sarah: bathroom (downstairs)
Brian: group leader
Joe: outside smoking area
Pat: living room and dining room
Jack: kitchen

Kitchen. Okay. What does that mean? Just clean it?

"Mel, am I just cleaning it? The kitchen?" I ask.

"Yeah, take out the rubbish, wipe down the sides, and wash up any cups and plates left in there and so on," she says.

I nod. I walk into the kitchen and it isn't too bad. There are a couple of plates on the side but the bin is full.

I take out the rubbish, come back inside and put a new bin bag in. I wash up the plates and I wipe the sides down.

Clean. Sorted. That was easy.

"How often do I do this?" I ask Mel.

"Three times a day," she says.

Okay, fine.

"We will be electing a group leader tonight. That person will wake up residents and set up the games room for meetings. Also they will show new residents the ropes," Mel says.

"Okay, it won't be me though," I say.

"Why not?"

"Well I have only been here a couple of days," I say.

"That doesn't matter! Brian is group leader at the moment. As you saw he isn't great at getting up so I'm sure he is eager to pass it on."

I laugh. Mel smiles. She has a lovely smile. I think I would like to be group leader. I wouldn't mind the responsibility. Something to get up for. Something to do.

I head to the toilet.

I am sick. It's painful and my chest burns.

I clean up and head out, over towards the sofas. I sit down and shut my eyes.

I hear Brian head out of the office and use the phone. I don't want to listen to his conversation as I don't want to intrude, so I get up and push the door shut.

He cries down the receiver. He laughs. He smiles.

I try not to look. I can't help being nosey, always been a bad habit of mine. He puts down the phone and enters the room I am in.

"Thanks for pulling the door shut, Jack," he says, wiping his eyes and sitting next to me.

"No problem, assumed you didn't want everyone listening," I say.

"You assume correct, Hendrix," he says smiling. "It's going to be all right, Jack you know. I feel different this time. Jane was saying that she is proud of me, I don't feel she should be but it felt nice to hear."

"Brian, you should be proud of yourself. It takes a lot to admit you need help and you did that. That is the hardest part. Now we need to be strong for the people we love," I say.

"Fuck me, where did that come from?" Brian says laughing and wiping his eyes again.

"Sorry," I say laughing. "That was a bit deep,

wasn't it?"

"Yeah but it was nice, love," Brian says, clapping me on the back.

Chapter 19: Visiting time

Been here a few days now. I am starting to feel better as the days go on. My stomach doesn't hurt as much as it usually does. Some of my energy has returned and I can now eat.

I am still being sick, but only really when I wake up. The shakes now come and go. It is kept vigilantly in control by Mike in the medical office. I am still having the vitamin jab in my arse cheek. It feels constantly bruised but I couldn't give a shit. It makes me feel so much better.

I got up early this morning and played some basketball in the garden. Such miniscule things as this, I feel so much pride in. I am going to get healthy. I can fucking do this. I can prove to myself that I can stick to something. I can't go back to how things were. It is worse than death and what's the point in dying when living feels this good.

I was alone on the basketball court. Breathing in the clean, fresh air and shutting my eyes. I loved the silence and the peace I felt. I felt like this is the start of something. The possibilities are literally endless now. I can live. Finally.

I am sitting in the living room, warm and comfortable.

Mel enters. "Jack how would you feel about being house leader?" she asks.

I honestly don't know how to feel about that. It means I have to wake the other residents in the morning etcetera.

"Yes, okay," I say. "Does no one else want to?"

"The other residents voted for you to be," she says, smiling.

"Unlucky!" Brian shouts across the room. I laugh.

I don't mind. I am sure to Brian it was a bit of a pain, but right now I need the distraction. I don't mind getting up early as I still am not sleeping too much.

"Thanks," I say to Mel.

She smiles and continues. "Also, today I am taking some residents up the road to the shop to get some food and bits. Do you fancy coming? It's only a five minute walk there?" she says.

"Yeah that sounds good!" I say. I feel butterflies in my stomach. They have drink there, I know this. I don't think of the drink in a 'I want to drink it' way. I think about it in a wary way. I know it's there and I need to be strong.

I head upstairs and have a shower. I get out, get changed and meet everyone downstairs. Only three residents can go with one staff member. It is me, Abbie and Joe.

Mel spots me. "All set, Jack?" she says.

"Yup," I say.

We exit the facility and walk down the brick steps into the car park. It has only been a few days but it already feels like so long ago, that I was being helped up these steps, with alcohol still on my breath, by my poor mum.

She is visiting today. This afternoon. I am nervous but very excited. I thought I would cry and beg to go home. That is what I was feeling yesterday. I woke up today feeling different. I don't know why.

We walk down the drive onto the country path. I look out onto a farm to the right of us as we make our way slowly towards the road. There is a barn with large parts of the roof ripped open. Pieces of it lay strewn across the path. Black and grey soot surrounds the outer wall of the barn.

"What happened here?" I ask Mel.

"There was a fire a few weeks ago!" she says. "We had to evacuate the facility, it was massive."

"Jesus…" I say, looking at the remains of torn metal and wood.

We reach the road and walk up for around three minutes. It feels very strange to be outside, in civilization. Cars pass, dog walkers walk, and I wonder if they know that we are patients at the facility. We have to wear fluorescent vests when we leave, so we stand out quite a bit. I don't care really.

We reach the shop and I stand outside finishing a cigarette.

"Now, Jack, there is alcohol inside. I don't expect that to be an issue, but if you feel like it's too much just let me know and I can get what you need. Okay?" Mel says.

I love her in this moment. I really appreciate her saying this. She doesn't have to, but she cares. It makes all the difference.

"Thanks, I'll be okay though I think," I say smiling.

Mel nods and I enter the shop. Immediately I see the alcohol section. It sticks out like a sore thumb and I have never noticed it this quickly before. I feel my heart sink and I feel anxious.

I am fine. I know I can do this, I am fine.

I walk over to the sweet and chocolate aisle and pick out some stuff I like. Since stopping drinking my sweet tooth has come back with a vengeance. I guess the amount of sugar in cider is extremely high, so my body is craving it.

I head over to the queue and stand for around a minute, keeping my eye line fixed away from the alcohol aisle and focusing on the person in front.

I pay for my bits and I leave the store.

I feel so good. Like I have just accomplished something big. Mel notices my smile as I leave.

"How you feeling?" she says, smiling.

"Great. I saw the alcohol but I didn't have the urge I used to. I guess I feel like what has happened has scared me so much, now I feel terrified of being near it," I say. "Which is a good thing…"

Mel smiles. "Exactly, Jack, that's exactly right. Well done for facing your fears and getting past it."

I do feel great. I walk back down the road with Abbie and Joe with Mel leading.

"Feels weird seeing drink again doesn't it?" Abbie says.

"Yeah," I say, "But I am glad I came."

"Good," Abbie says smiling at me.

We walk in silence back to the dirt path. The wind beats down on us as we trudge toward Bridge House and I think about seeing my family. It makes my heart jump and I can't wait. I am also proud that I have been made house leader. I have always had a feeling I am not a nice person, that there is something inherently wrong with me and I have never been able to figure out what. Maybe I feel I am too much, not enough. I don't know, but the fact these people who have only known me a few days have decided to have me wake them up and set up meetings makes me feel I may have made a good impression.

We arrive back and I head towards the kitchen. I have bought some sweets, chocolate and fizzy drink. I am craving that feeling of the fizz. I don't know whether that is a good or bad thing but I don't care. I grab a cup from the cupboard and I pour myself a large glass.

I stand at the sink and I drain the contents. Almost immediately my anxiety dissipates and I feel better. I don't know why that is. I just feel better.

I head into the dining room and walk out through the doors leading to the garden. A few of the residents stand outside smoking.

I sit down and I roll a cigarette. I light up and inhale. I feel fucking amazing today. This always seems to happen. I feel terrible and then fantastic, it's always up and down. I don't care why, I am just enjoying this feeling.

"You got any visitors, love?" Brian asks.

"Yeah, my mum's coming I think," I say smiling.

"You two get on well?" he asks.

"Yeah, pretty well. I have treated her like shit though, I don't deserve her really," I say embarrassed.

"She sounds like a good woman," he says, looking out over the garden.

"Yeah, she's pretty amazing," I say. I stub out my cigarette. I pat Brian on the back and head inside.

My mum should be arriving soon. I head upstairs and go to my room. I open the door and I make my bed. I put my clothes that are thrown around my room back in the cupboard and I sit on my bed. I smell bad even though I had a shower not long ago. I keep sweating a lot, due to the withdrawal.

I realise everyone is waiting outside the medical room and I head over to them and stand waiting.

"You got anyone coming?" I ask Abbie.

"Nope," she says.

"Your mum or anyone?" I say.

"She's dead. So is my dad, haven't got anyone," she replies, staring at the blank wall.

"I'm sorry, Abbie… I didn't know, sorry," I say.

"Don't be, you didn't kill her," she says, before heading into the medical room.

I wonder what she meant by that. I don't focus too much on it and I wait for my turn. It comes and I head into the medical room. Abbie smiles at me when she leaves.

Dev stands with his back to me.

"You're back!" I say happily.

"Jack, mate, how are you? Feeling a lot better? I hear you have made house leader. You have made quite the impression on the others," he says smiling, eyebrows raised.

"Really? I don't think I have, I think they have to give it to someone and just gave it to me because I am new," I say, feeling embarrassed.

"Nah, man, Abbie was just saying how lovely you are, you may have to watch out for her," he says, winking and laughing.

I go a deep red. "Oh right…" I laugh with him.

"So, you need your jab," he says. "I feel so bad I have to give it to you but it helps a lot."

"Honestly I don't mind, it makes me feel better," I say, smiling.

"You have to be the first person to say that," he replies, laughing.

I stand up and drop my pants.

"Hang on, mate, I need to give you your tablets first!" he says.

"Oh shit," I say laughing and pulling up my trousers.

"Cor, buy me a drink first…" he says, laughing.

I laugh and wait. He turns around and hands me my tablets. There aren't as many as usual.

"Why isn't there as much in here?" I ask concerned.

"Yeah, that stuff can be addictive, so we take you off it slowly. As your withdrawals decrease," he says.

"Right, yeah that makes sense," I say.

I take the tablets and wait. Dev sorts out the needle and instructs me to stand and he gives me the injection. Again, painful, but worth it.

"Okay, mate! I'll see you later, take care yeah?" he says and I smile.

"You too, Dev, see you later." I leave and head to my room. I grab my towel and head to the shower room.

I have a wash and decide to shave. By this point I have horrible long stubble on my face and I want to start to look a bit better.

I shave and head out. I go to my room and get changed. I see some cars pulling into the car park. I look out and see my mum's pulling into the far space. The butterflies in my stomach return and I make my way downstairs.

I stand apprehensively in the corridor just beyond the entrance. I wait to hear my mum's voice. I feel nervous. I don't know why.

I hear voices in the reception. I don't hear my mum. The voices are apparently owned by Craig's family, coming to see him. I wait for a few more minutes and hear new footsteps. I hear my mum's voice and I smile. She is with someone.

Mel comes into the corridor where I stand waiting.

"Jack, some people are here to see you!" she says smiling.

I smile back and my mum comes through the door, followed by my little brother Ben. I cry. I walk up to my mum and I hug her. She cries. My brother joins our hug.

"Hey, Mum…" I say, trying to fight back the barrage of tears.

"Hey, Jacko, how are you?" she asks. "You look so well, love!"

"Hey, mate! I missed you!" my brother says, embracing me tightly.

"God, I missed you both. It's only been a few days but feels like longer," I reply. "I am a lot better than the last time you saw me."

"Jacko, I am so proud of you," my mum says, hugging me again.

"Thank you…" I say, I can't stop the tears. I feel so emotional. "Anyway! Shall I show you around?"

"Yes please!" my mum says. My brother is smiling and I am so happy to see them both.

I take them through to the living room and introduce them to some of the other residents. I keep it short and sweet because I know everyone here doesn't feel great and meeting new people is stressful. I show them the garden. We walk around it. I show my mum and brother the basketball court. I tell them I have played and it feels good to be able to do stuff. They smile proudly.

We walk back inside and head towards the games room. I ask if they would like a coffee or a tea and they say they are fine. I pull up three chairs in the games room and we sit down.

"I can't believe you guys are here. This whole thing is so surreal," I say. Now I can't stop smiling.

"Darling, look at you. The colour in your face is already returning. Are you feeling better than the other day?" my mum says, smiling.

"I am sorry about that I just…"

"Don't be sorry," she says. "You stuck at it and you're doing so well."

"I am so proud of you, mate. You look like a new person!" my brother says. He looks as though he may cry. This moves me. He is very similar to me, we are both very emotional people. He has a heart of gold and kept me company so many times when I felt alone and desperate.

"Thanks, man," I say. "This is the games room. I play pool in here sometimes. I felt like shit yesterday but today I feel slightly better. Well, a lot better today. This has made me so happy…"

My mum and brother smile broadly. I smile back.

"So tell us everything so far love," my mum says excitably.

I tell them about the first day. How I cried for hours, but knew that I had to be there, had to stay and fight through the terror I felt. I tell them about the writing on the whiteboard in my room, how it gave me strength to repeat those words to myself. I tell them about Brian, Abbie, Joe and the other residents. About Mike, Tom, Mel and Dev. I explain that Dev helped me in the middle of the night when I thought I was alone. The amazing talk we had that helped me sleep for the first time in such a long time.

"I am house leader as well..." I say.

"*What*?" My mum says loudly, looking very happy.

"Yeah, I think it's a normal thing here but I have to wake up the other residents in the morning, show new residents around and set up the meetings," I say.

"Jack. If you could go back and tell yourself last week, what you're telling me now, would you believe it?"

I smile at the thought. "No, I wouldn't. I wouldn't at all."

My mum looks at my brother and they both laugh. I start laughing too.

"Can you show us your room?" my mum says.

"I think so? I'm sure its fine," I say.

We get up and walk out of the games room and head towards the stairs. We walk up and my mum and brother comment on how lovely the place is.

"It's like a country house!" my brother says.

"I know," I say, smiling again.

We reach the corridor and I show them the bathroom and shower room. I lead them to my room and we walk inside. It's messy, but I am not embarrassed.

"Jack, this isn't bad at all is it?" my mum says, looking around the room in shock.

"I know, it's great," I say, sitting on my bed and exhaling.

"I love the fact you did this, Jack, it proves that you want this," my brother says pointing at the white board.

"I do want it, very much," I say smiling.

"We haven't got long, love, as I have to get back to do the horses," my mum says, looking apologetic.

I understand, she needs to feed them and put them into the stables she rents etcetera.

"Don't worry at all, it was just so lovely to see you," I tell my mum.

I get up and hug her and then hug my brother. We walk downstairs and I tell my mum about my trip to the shops. I tell her how nice it was to walk into an off license and not buy alcohol. She smiles and hugs me as we walk.

"I am so proud of you, I knew you could do this Jack," my mum says.

We reach the hallway downstairs and I follow them out to reception. I embrace them both and feel like I don't want to let go.

"You stay strong, my darling," my mum says as she hugs me.

"I will, I promise I will," I say back.

"So proud of you, Jacko, we are all behind you, Always," my brother says.

"Thank you both so much, it meant the world to me you guys coming here," I say, feeling as though I may cry again. I don't though. I hold back tears and wave them off smiling. I feel so much love and support I feel invincible.

I walk back into the corridor, head through the living room, out into the garden. It's cold. I zip up my jacket and I sit down. I can't wipe this smile from my face. I don't know what I would do without my family. They give me so much strength.

I have so much respect and admiration for those who go through this without a family. It takes true guts and must be beyond difficult. I spark up a cigarette and think about the others inside who have no one. I feel so much sadness and pain for them. I can't imagine how difficult and scary this must be to go through alone.

I smoke and I look into the dark sky. The air is still and I see my breath evaporate in a cloud of mist as I exhale. I think about the words my mum and brother said to me. I think about their journey home, knowing I am safe and getting better.

Today has been one of the good ones. I won't forget it.

Chapter 20: farewell alcohol

"Brian, wake up, mate," I say, knocking on his door hard. It is eight o'clock in the morning. I have been waking the residents up for a couple of days and Brian is proving to be a bloody nightmare. He just doesn't want to get up in the mornings. I know that I have felt this way when I have been depressed but it helps to get up and start your day.

"Fuck meee, I am up!" I hear him say, his voice muffled by his duvet.

"Sweet, see you in a bit."

I head to the other residents' doors and knock lightly, telling them it is time to get up for meds. They all respond; most of them just grunt but at least it acknowledges they have heard me.

I head to the medical room and get my meds given to me by Mike. I swallow them, get my jab and leave. I head downstairs. I make myself a coffee in the kitchen and go outside for a cigarette. Snow lies on the ground and blankets the garden in a fantastic white sheet. I brush off some of the snow on a bench and I sit. I smoke my cigarette in silence.

I see Tom walking towards me. He opens the door to the garden and comes outside.

"Jack, how are we today? Everyone up?"

"Yup, Brian took a while," I say, smiling.

"Yeah, he normally does. Listen today we have a new resident coming in. He is called Sid and is arriving at one. You okay to make him feel at home after all the usual stuff like introduction etcetera?" he says.

I chuck my cigarette on the floor and nod. "Yeah sure. How old is he?" I ask.

"Older than you," Tom says, smiling. He always seems to feel funny about saying anything about new residents before I meet them or they turn up. I guess he wants their information to stay private.

"Right, okay." I laugh.

"We have a group this morning, can you make sure the room is clear and let everyone know? It's at eleven o'clock," Tom says. He turns and makes his way inside.

"Yup," I say.

I drink some of my coffee, get up, and walk inside. Most of the residents are downstairs potting about.

"Guys, we have a new resident coming today. Also there is group at eleven in the games room," I say to the room.

A few of the residents acknowledge what I have said and Abbie speaks.

"Who's the new guy?"

"His name is Sid, that's all I know," I say, sitting myself down on the sofa.

"Okay, wonder if he will be like the last one," she says, looking at the TV.

None of us have heard anything about Paul. I didn't really want to ask in case it was bad news, it scared the shit out of me.

"I'm sure he will be fine," I say, drinking my coffee.

We watch TV for a while and Brian emerges downstairs.

"You'll be the death of me, babe," He mutters to me as he passes in front of the TV.

"I have to wake you, you know that," I say, laughing.

He smiles back and laughs too. "I know, I'm fucking useless in the mornings," he says.

"Yeah, I think most people are," I say.

Brian gets himself a coffee and heads over to the dining table and starts his colouring in.

"Why do you do that so much?" I say, laughing.

"It relaxes me love," he replies, not looking up.

"Fair enough," I say.

I get up and go upstairs. I have a shower and get changed into some jogging bottoms and a jumper. I go to my room and grab my journal. I write in it about the past few days. It's not that interesting, but I want to look back on it and be able to remember where I was and what I was feeling. I put my notepad and look out of the window. It has started snowing again. I hear noise out in the garden.

I head back downstairs and realise everyone is outside, apparently playing in the snow.

I head towards the back door, open it, and get a snowball straight in my face. It's freezing cold and falls down my jumper turning my back to ice.

"Fuck!" I shout.

"Sorry, love…" I hear Brian say, as another snowball skims my head.

I laugh a lot. I can't see him, I think he is behind a bush.

I sneak around it and plant a snowball right in his face.

"Jesus!" he shouts. We laugh hard. I help him up and we go walking around the garden. It is beautiful. The snow is untouched on the basketball court and on the pond next to it. I look inside and see carp swimming around. I sit on the edge and watch.

"So you said you've been here before?" I ask Brian, who in turn has perched on the edge of the pond.

"Yeah. Couple of years ago," he says. He too is watching the fish meander around the black depths of the pond. "It wasn't under the same circumstances though."

"Oh right," I reply, looking up at him. "What happened?"

"Me and my wife had taken some time apart. I was in a bad place and didn't know what to do really. I just drank, every day, until I couldn't think about it," he says. He gets up and brushes his trousers of the snow and wipes his hands on his coat.

"I know the feeling. Not the part about your wife, but drinking to not feel anything," I say.

"You're so young though, love! Surely there can't be anything that bad worth forgetting..." he says looking at me.

"Maybe there isn't, I don't know, I just can't deal with my thoughts. I think horrible things about myself and I can't control it. I feel like I don't deserve to be alive a lot of the time," I say. I look down at the fish and a tear drops off my cheek into the water.

The fish swim up and around, picking at bits of plants on the surface.

"I can understand that. I think a lot of people here can understand that, love. I think you're more intelligent than you give yourself credit for Jack," he says, sitting next to me.

"How so?" I say back, not looking at him.

"You knew you had a problem and you wanted to fix it. Not just for yourself but for those around you. You're so young and you took responsibility for something most adults would struggle to even think about," he says, patting me on the back.

"I had to. It was killing my mum, and the rest of my family." I wipe my eyes and look at Brian. "I just don't want to fuck this up, I want to finish this and put it behind me."

"I believe you will, Jack," Brian says, smiling. "If I can do it, you sure as shit can, okay?"

I nod my head and stand. "Thanks, Brian," I say, I hug him.

"Course, love, don't let them see you hugging me they may think I'm grooming you…"

"Fucks sake…" I say, laughing hard.

We walk back to the house and head into the living room. I thank Brian again. He makes a face as if to say, 'don't mention it' and he sits down on the sofa. I head out of the living room and into the games room. I start pulling the chairs off the wall where they are propped up. The room is cold and grey; I switch the lights on and turn the nozzles on the radiators to get some heating.

People file in and I take a seat in my normal place. Tom comes in last and addresses us.

"Everybody okay? Is everyone here?"

We all nod and he continues.

"Today I want us to do something different. I want you all to write a letter to alcohol. I want you to make peace with the things that happened and say goodbye to the pain and madness alcohol caused; this is your goodbye letter to the substance that brought you here," he says.

I like the sound of this. I kind of like writing anyway, this is interesting.

"We tend to romanticise our time with alcohol. So in this way, we get to say goodbye to it. I want you all to take half an hour and write out your letters," he says.

Tom stands up and hands us all a blank piece of paper and a pen each. We disperse and some of us leave the room, Brian and Pat stay behind to write theirs. I head up to my room. I want privacy to write it.

I sit down on my bed and I stare at the whiteboard. I look at the words that were scribbled on there in a moment of pure terror and panic. I think about whether things could've ever been different. Whether I could've ever not ended up here.

I begin to write.

Dear alcohol.

Sometimes I wonder whether it was you or me who was in the wrong. I think about the things I have done when under your spell and it is so unlike me. We had good times but ultimately they had to come to an end. You broke my will and my character. I am not the same person anymore. I don't think I hate you for that.

I wish I could've been like everyone else. I wish I could've enjoyed our time and not become so attached. Ultimately I cannot change what has happened, but in order for me to continue my life, I have to do this without you in it. I need control again, I need to take back the reins and steer myself in the right direction. It's been you driving this whole time and it's been a wild ride on an inevitable collision course towards death and destruction. I can't do it anymore, I am too tired. My spark has been extinguished by you, and now I am left in the dark searching for answers.

Life is too important, family is too special, and I now realise I was wrong to trust in you. I want to say goodbye.

I know others will enjoy your company for many years to come but for me it's the wrong company to keep. I am wired differently, it won't ever work. I need to strive to find the person I was before, without your influence.

Insanity is the process of doing the same thing over and over again, expecting a different result.

I am not insane.

At least I am not anymore.

Goodbye.

I look over my writing. I realise as I am writing, it's like I am writing to someone I loved. It kind of makes sense though. I am happy with it. It really sums up how I feel and that's all that matters.

I fold the piece of paper and write my name on it. I tuck it in my inside pocket of my jacket and head downstairs. I still have ten minutes until I have to go back. I go outside.

I sit on a bench and roll a cigarette. I spark up and sit watching the others through the living room windows. All deep in thought, some laughing to each other.

I look in the games room and see Pat and Brian, heads down, writing. They probably wanted privacy like me.

I head back inside and sit on a chair at the dining table. Tom comes in and asks us to come into the games room and we all stand and follow him.

"So I see some of you have written a lot, others not much. I think because of time I will ask a couple of you to read yours out. Who would like to start?"

I raise my hand, so do Brian and Abbie.

"Brian?" Tom says.

Brian nods his head and prepares to read.

"To wine, vodka and all your mates that I hate.

"Fuck you. I despise you. You are a bitch. I almost lost everything because of you and things have been hell since you took over my life.

"My wife has been put through the worst things because of you. I haven't seen my newborn child because of what you have done to me. Fuck you.

"I will no more let you rule my life.

"I'm done, babes.

Yours sincerely, fuck off."

Brian looks up, tears in his eyes but a smile on his face. We all laugh and Tom speaks.

"Well, that was good, Brian. Slightly expletive but that's understandable. I especially like the 'and all your mates' part. You also touched on real things that were affected by alcohol and your addiction. It was great, Brian, well done."

We all agree and say well done to Brian and he blow kisses at us all.

"Can I go next?" Abbie says.

"Yes, of course," Tom replies.

Abbie isn't smiling. She isn't enjoying this and I can tell that this has been quite difficult for her.

"I have been trying to figure out how to put this down into words.

"Hate isn't close. I am terrified of you.

"I am scared of everything you represent. The fact you are so accepted in our normal everyday society but you destroy so many people's lives. I have been physically abused, attacked and broken by someone also addicted to you. I turned to you to comfort me throughout what happened to me. You destroyed me like you destroyed him.

"I can't stand it anymore and I want out.

"I want to have a good life and can't with you in it.

"Bye, alcohol."

Abbie is crying. She buries her face in her hands and Pat puts her arm over her and comforts her.

I can't look at her, it upsets me seeing her cry. I stare at the floor and think about what Abbie wrote and feel for her.

"Thank you for sharing that, Abbie," Tom says. "We have spoken about your story and you know how shocked I was about everything that happened to you, that took guts to write that, Abbie."

Abbie nods her head, face still buried in her hands and she cries hard.

We all say thank you to Abbie for sharing and Tom continues.

"This is why I wanted us to do this. I knew it would stir up some hard feelings and memories, but it's important to know the facts and what it did to you. It's part of accepting the past and moving on with knowledge you now have."

I nod my head. "Can I go next" I ask.

"Yeah, of course, Jack, if no one else minds?"

We look around and everyone nods and I start.

I finish and feel emotional after reading my letter aloud. I look up and Tom looks like he is in deep thought.

"That was brilliant, Jack. Almost like you were talking to an ex-partner. I was very interested that you used the words 'Dear alcohol'." He smiles and I laugh.

"I don't know, I just start letters that way…" I say.

"Yeah, of course," Tom says smiling. "The part about insanity was very, very true. We actually use that saying in recovery to describe relapse. We always think things will be different, we tell ourselves that things will be better this time around, when they never are," he says.

"Yeah, I think someone in CRI told me that before I came here. I guess it just stuck with me," I say shrugging.

"Well it was great to hear that, Jack, thank you," Tom says, smiling.

"Thanks," I say, nodding. Brian pats me on the back and Abbie smiles empathetically at me.

"What I want you to do now is a bit odd. I want you all to go outside and burn the letters. You have said your piece, now it is time to let go of it," Tom says.

"Do we have to? I kind of liked what I wrote…" I say, and everyone laughs.

"Yes, Jack," Tom says laughing. "It is important. You have said how you feel and what is on your mind, but alcohol can't read your letter; the important thing was getting the words out and moving on after saying how you feel. It is a way of saying goodbye and ridding yourself of these feelings and questions in your head."

I don't know about this. I will burn it, but I don't think I will be rid of my feelings and thoughts about it. I get it though. The letter is a metaphor, I guess. I nod my head and everyone stands up and we walk to the garden.

We stand on the patio outside the garden doors and Tom brings out a metal bin. He puts it in the middle of us and asks us to light our letters on fire and throw them into the bin.

"Okay, Pat, do you want to start," Tom says.

Pat, saying nothing, lights her letter and throws it into the bin. One after another we light our letters and throw them in. I stand by the bin watching my letter burn and think in my head, *Good riddance*. I have said what I need to say and now it is done.

I spark up a cigarette and watch. The others do the same.

"You think this will work?" I ask Brian.

"Worth a go, innit, babes," he says back, chucking his cigarette into the bin. I do the same and we walk inside. I sit down and turn on the TV. Brian joins me and we sit and watch television for a while waiting for lunch.

Chapter 21: Sid

We all sit down and eat lunch. Today it is chicken and bacon pasta bake. It tastes incredible. I eat a lot. We chat around the table.

"So what time is this new guy arriving?" I ask.

Mel looks up and thinks.

"Twelve-thirty? I need to check with Tom," she replies.

"What do I do when he arrives?" I ask.

"Nothing to begin with. He will have drunk alcohol so we need to separate him from you guys for the afternoon. Then, as we did with you, we will bring him down and you can introduce him to the others," Mel says, smiling.

"Oh gawd," I say, finishing off my pasta and standing up.

"You'll be fine, Jack," Mel says, laughing.

I put my plate on the trolley and smile back at Mel. I go over to the sofa and slump down into it. I feel tired and anxious again. Always happens after eating.

I write in my journal about the day. I shut the journal, close my eyes and try to have a nap.

I wake up around an hour later. Mel has tapped me on the shoulder.

"Sid has arrived, Jack, we are taking him upstairs now."

"Right, okay, thanks," I say.

I look over to the stairs and see a very skinny, frail man. He looks to be in his late forties. His eyes have great, dark rings around them and he has a yellowish tinge to his skin. I smell alcohol waft through the living room door; I hold my breath and recoil.

He is helped up the stairs by Mike and Tom, legs shaking, trying his best to put one foot in front of the other. I feel for him. I know that feeling. Pure anxiety and panic flood my senses as I think about this. I try to put it out of my mind. Luckily, I am past the worst of the withdrawals. The sickness has eased, my shaking is little to non-existent and I am eating and sleeping pretty normally. I still can't even believe this as I think it. Just feels unreal.

I get up and head over to the dining table. Brian and Abbie are playing cards.

"What are you guys up to?" I ask, sitting myself down next to Abbie.

"Playing cheat, love," Brian says, looking at his cards.

"Nice," I say. "Can I play tonight?"

"Yes, babe, of course," Abbie says, looking at me and smiling. I smile back. I get up and go up to my room. I still feel exhausted after eating, I need to sleep. I get to the upstairs landing and see Mike and Tom talking in the corridor. They look concerned.

"Hey," I say, passing them to go to my room.

"Hi, Jack," Tom says.

I enter my room, shut the door, draw the blinds and lay my head down on the pillow. It is cold. I like it. I shut my eyes and exhale.

I am in a bright room. There is a ball of black mass in the middle of the room. I look down and see my feet. I feel a burning urge to drink. I want to drink as much as I can. As I feel this, the mass gets larger. It shakes violently and becomes more aggressive. I feel a bottle in my hand. It is a clear, ice cold bottle of vodka. I try to open the bottle. I can't get it open. I smash it on the floor. It breaks. I shove the bottle into my mouth, I drink, drink, drink. I feel nothing. I feel sick. I feel the vomit inducing burning in my stomach. I cry out. The mass is unstable. The mass screams. It explodes. I wake up.

I am soaked in sweat and my door is open.

"Jack? You okay?" Dev stands above me. I am shaking and I feel sick. I get up and I launch myself towards the bin in my room and I vomit.

"Fuck," I moan into the bin. I feel drunk, dizzy and anxious. "I thought I was done with being sick."

"You missed your medication, mate, I was coming to find you and heard you moaning," he says, helping me to my feet.

"I feel awful," I say, I am hot and feel sick.

"Come with me, let's get you some Librium," he says. I follow him out of my room. I feel my face drenched in sweat and its cold as the air hits my forehead.

We enter the medication room and I sit down. This isn't as bad as before. I don't feel like I am going to hallucinate, I just feel dazed and sick. Dev hands me my medication and I take it fast.

"Give it half hour, you'll feel better," he says.

I nod my head and shut my eyes. "I haven't had my injection today," I say.

Dev looks at a clip board and nods.

"Okay, no worries."

I stand up and Dev gives me the injection. I thank him and leave the room. I head back into my bedroom and change into some comfy clothes. I am already starting to feel better.

I head downstairs and enter the living room. Sid is sitting outside, I can see him through the window. I sit down and start to roll a cigarette.

"You look rough," Abbie says, smiling and sitting down next to me on the sofa.

"Yeah, I had a horrible fucking dream," I say.

"Drinking?" she says, smiling; I look at her and smile back.

"How did you know? Is that normal?" I say.

"Yeeeees. I've had it most nights. It does get less intense don't worry," she says, grabbing my rizla and tobacco, continuing to roll my cigarette for me. She can tell I am shaking and I appreciate this.

"Thanks," I say smiling.

"No problem…" she says.

"So what is he like?" I say, motioning my head over to Sid outside.

"Hasn't really said much, think he is a bit out of it, and most likely quite nervous." Abbie replies.

I nod my head and she passes my cigarette. She begins rolling her own.

"I feel bad, I wasn't up when he came downstairs…" I say.

"Nah, don't worry about it, he had Mel with him." Abbie says, licking the paper of the roll up cigarette and fastening it in a tight tube. "Shall we?" she says, smiling and getting up.

I stand up and follow her into the garden. I notice Brian is outside with Sid. Shit. He is probably driving him fucking nuts. We walk out and go over to them.

"Hi, I'm Jack, Sid, isn't it?" I say holding out my hand. Sid takes it and shakes extremely softly. His hand is sweaty. He is visibly shaking and looks exhausted.

"Hi," he says, extremely quietly.

"Bet you don't feel great at all. Don't worry, that does get easier. I am the house leader which means if you need to know anything about resident stuff just give me a shout. I don't bite and I'm happy to help, I know how scary this can be."

Sid nods and smiles. I smile back and sit down to have my cigarette.

"You're sweet," Abbie says.

"Nah, I'm a bastard really," I say, smiling. We both laugh and watch Brian talking Sid's ear off, apparently about his colouring…

They both head inside and we follow. Sid seems extremely fragile at this moment.

"I'm gonna go upstairs and get some sleep," he says to me.

"Okay, mate, make sure you leave your door slightly open so the staff can check on you," I say. He nods and makes his way up to his room. I head into the games room and rack up the pool table. I start hitting the balls around and Abbie comes in. She sits down. She watches me and smiles. I look up and smile back.

"Want to play?" I ask.

"Nah you're all right, I'll watch you…" she says smiling.

I shrug. "So when do you leave?" I ask.

"Same day as you," she says.

"Oh really? That's not long now"

"Yeah, I know…" she says, flicking through a book she has picked up from the stack close to her. "Can we stay in touch when we leave?"

I think about this. We have been told we aren't allowed to give out our numbers etcetera.

"Yeah, fuck it, why not," I say, grinning. She smiles warmly back at me.

"I like you, Jack. Not necessarily like that, but you're a nice person."

I feel myself going red. "Honestly if you knew me you wouldn't be saying that," I say, looking down and hitting some balls together on the table.

"How so? We have all done things we aren't proud of," she says, looking at me.

I keep my eyes on the table. I am nervous. I don't know why. I feel like she doesn't know me. It feels a bit strange her asking to stay in touch.

"Yeah, but I don't know, I just don't think I would be a great person to stay in contact with," I say.

She stays quiet and stares into the book she is holding.

"I think I want to make my mind up about that on my own," she says quietly.

I laugh and she laughs. "Okay, I'll give you my number before I leave. We can go for coffee or something. Speak about sober stuff," I say.

She grins widely. "Yes, that sounds good."

She gets up and walks out of the room not saying anything else. I don't feel for her in 'that' way, but I do like her. I just get worried about seeing another addict outside of here. It can go either way really. Either you help each other, or the opposite.

I put the pool cue down against the wall and I walk out and up the stairs to my room. I head to the medical room for my medication. I hear retching and moaning. I pass by a room with its door ajar and I can't help but see inside.

Sid is on his knees, throwing up violently into the bin next to his bed. His torso is bruised and frail. He has a shaved head and I see on the back of his head cuts and bruises. He is wearing stained pants and nothing else and rocks to and fro by the bin. The room smells so bad. I hold my breath. I knock.

"Sid, everything all right? Can I get someone for you?" I say softly through the small open part of the door.

He doesn't reply for a moment. He breathes in deeply and exhales heavily.

"I don't know," he responds. His voice is shaking and he sounds upset.

"Hang on, mate, I'll grab someone, you're going to be all right."

I go over to the medical room and I knock on the door rapidly. Mike answers.

"Mike, Sid's not doing well at all, can you check on him?" I say, looking concerned.

"I was just about to, mate, is he okay?" he says coming out of the doorway and shutting it behind him, locking it up.

"He is being sick and sounds bad," I say.

"Okay, thanks, Jack."

I stand where I am and Mike heads over to his door. He pushes it opens and goes inside the room. I listen for a moment, and then walk into my room.

I sit on my bed, open a bag of sweets and eat some. I write in my journal about Sid and everything today that's happened so far. I stare at the writing on my whiteboard and I get up and go downstairs.

I go over to the sofas and sit down. I can hear Pat in the other room. She is asking Abbie for her number. I have heard her asking a few times now, and Abbie keeps making excuses. Pat apparently has something called 'wet brain'. Brian told me yesterday that the amount of alcohol she has used over the years has affected her mind. She tends to ask a lot of questions over and over again and gets very confused, much of the time.

I feel lucky to have not developed that. There is so much I am still learning about what alcohol can do to you if you are addicted to it. It is terrifying.

I get up and head outside. There is snow everywhere still and I walk across an untouched patch on the grass. I head over to the swings. I sit down and I start moving backwards and forwards. The wood creaks as I swing. I notice Brian's face in the games room window. I smile. He seems to be laughing at me. I don't care. I feel so relaxed and can't remember the last time I was on one of these.

Abbie and Craig's faces pop up in the other windows of the games room and everyone is laughing. I start laughing too. I must look very odd right now. I try to jump off the seat mid swing and balls up my landing. I splat face down in the snow and wind myself.

I get up wheezing and can hear Brian laughing from where I am. I try to laugh too but all the air has jumped out of my chest. I walk back to the patio area, sit down and roll a cigarette.

The others come outside, still laughing.

"You're fucking hilarious…" Brian says, sitting down to the left of me. I laugh.

"I wasn't trying to be, I was genuinely having fun," I say.

Abbie, Brian and Craig continue laughing. I laugh too.

"My wife is coming to see me tonight…" Brian says.

"Oh really, you excited?" I ask.

"Can't wait," he replies.

"What time they getting here?"

"After dinner I think," he says.

I nod and smile. I wonder what she looks like. I bet she is very nice. From the sounds of things she is pretty great. I get up and head back inside. Mel is talking to Pat and Joe. I approach them and Joe turns to me.

"You coming to acupuncture?" he asks.

I have heard of it but never experienced it. "Maybe, what does it entail?" I ask.

Mel turns and speaks. "I basically put very small needles in pressure points in your ears. It helps a lot with anxiety and relaxation."

"Yeah, I'm up for that…" I say.

"Great! Let's just wait for the others and see if they fancy it," she says.

Brian, Abbie and Craig come back into the dining room and Mel asks them if they fancy it. Abbie follows Mel; Brian and Craig sit down at the dinner table.

"Okay, follow me!" Mel says to me, Joe and Pat. We follow her and Abbie up the stairs, to the room where I did the guided meditation. We walk in and Mel asks us to sit down. There are four chairs in a circle centred in the middle of the room.

I sit down and the others do the same. Mel heads over to a table. There are clear plastic bags with needles inside. She takes them and comes over to us.

"Okay, so I am going to put these in your pressure points in your ears," she says, "It doesn't hurt, it will feel maybe a bit uncomfortable at first, but it isn't painful."

I watch as she proceeds to place the needles on Joe. It looks very weird. I am quite sceptical about this. Mel makes her way round the group, placing the needles very carefully in a pattern around the inner part of everyone ears. She reaches me, takes the plastic bag and removes the contents.

"Okay, Jack, this won't hurt," she says. She is very close to my face. I feel myself blushing.

She places the needles carefully in position. It feels odd. I feel pressure, a small irritable itch, but no pain. Once she is finished I have a strong urge to touch them, Mel sees me go to do this and tells me not to.

She walks over to the CD player and presses play. She switches off the lights and we are submerged in darkness. The music plays, slow and magical. It is relaxing.

"So, as we have done before, I will take you through some guided meditation."

I see others shut their eyes and I do the same. It is very quiet apart from Mel's voice and the soothing music.

"You are on a path. The path leads into some woods. You follow the path. It begins to get darker and darker and you are traveling deeper and deeper."

I am visualizing this. I am entering woods I remember from when I was child. The trees tower above me and a light breeze pushes them backwards and forwards, creating a chorus of rushing sounds all around me.

"You are deep in these woods. You see something in the distance. You try to make it out. As you get closer you see it is a crystal clear pool of water. You get undressed and proceed to enter the pool. It is warm and still. You float in the water and a break in the trees above forces sunlight down upon you. You lay there, effortlessly held by the clear water. It is warm and you are safe."

I can feel myself getting sleepy. I feel very relaxed. I am surprised by this. My ears are hot where the needles sit. It doesn't hurt. It feels good.

"You hear a noise from a clearing in front of you. You look and see a deer, bending its neck down to eat.

You stare at it, it does not notice you."
 I imagine this. I feel tired. I feel safe. I feel good. This is relaxing. I could die here and be happy.

Chapter 22: Sharing is caring

I wake up. I don't remember where I am. It is dark and music is playing. I feel something in my ears and I put my hand up to touch it. I hit the needles in my ears and feel pain.

"Fuck!" I shout. Everyone starts laughing. I remember where I am now. I forgot about the acupuncture. For a moment I thought I was back home. That's the most relaxed I have been in a long time.

"Sorry," I say quietly.

"You were snoring," Abbie says. I can hear her laughing.

"Fuck, that's bad, sorry," I say, embarrassed.

Mel flicks the light on and turns the music down. She is also laughing, as is Joe. Pat is still asleep.

"I can't believe it worked," I say to Mel.

She grins and passes me to wake Pat. "You were out for the count! How you feeling?" she asks.

"Great," I say. "Tired.

She gently taps Pat and she stirs and then wakes. She looks exhausted.

"I think they are serving dinner now if you all want to make your way down. I will take out the needles first," she says, looking at me.

"Yeah, sorry I forgot where I was, think I tried to take them out," I say.

She comes over to me and removes them. My ears still feel hot. I hope they do this again before I leave. I really did enjoy that. I get up and walk over to the door and exit. I head downstairs and can smell food. My mouth waters and I only just realise how starving hungry I am.

I head over to the trolley and pick up a plate. I load up on pasta, garlic bread and salad. Tom is sitting at the far end with Craig and Brian. I don't see Sid.

"Jack, how did you find the acupuncture?" Tom asks. Brian and Craig look over at me too.

"Actually so good. That's the most relaxed I have been in a long time," I say, sitting down next to Brian.

"Yeah, I have done it a couple of times. Really helps with anxiety, babe," Brian says.

I nod. "Tom, how is Sid?" I ask.

"He is still not great. I think he is sleeping at the moment so I have left him to it. Got people checking on him," he says.

"Okay, do I need to do anything?" I ask. Tom shakes his head and eats a mouthful of garlic bread. I shrug and begin eating.

It has started snowing again. A couple of the residents get up and look out the windows. I don't. I like the snow but I like my food better. I have started feeling like I've got more energy. I still struggle to sleep without extreme nightmares. They are vivid and terrifying. I can't get the ball of mass nightmare out of my head. I am scared to ask a member of staff about it. I am worried about what it means. I am worried I will sound mad. For the time being I keep it to myself.

I get up and place my plate in the usual place.

"Jack, we have a psychiatrist coming in tomorrow morning. She works with our residents once a week. Would you like me to ask her to see you?" Tom asks. It's like he was reading my mind.

"Yes. Please," I say back. This is exciting to me. I have always looked for the answer of what is wrong with me. If she can help me, it would be amazing. Maybe she can tell me what this recurring nightmare is about. I don't know, either way it will be nice to talk to someone.

"No problem, Jack, leave it with me."

"Sure," I say.

I head outside and roll a cigarette. I sit down and spark it up. I can hear crying. I don't know where from. It sounds muffled. I look up and try to pinpoint the noise.

It's coming from the medical room. It's Sid, I think. He is wailing loudly. I hear Mike consoling him. I feel bad for listening. I shouldn't listen.

"Am I going to die? I can't sleep, and I keep fucking throwing up," I hear him say.

I don't hear Mike's reply. I know how Sid feels. It hurts to think about him feeling the way I felt. I want to help. I really want to fucking help. What can I do?

Nothing. I am just a few stages ahead of him coming off alcohol. I can't do anything. I am a resident here just like he is. This makes me angry and sad. I'm sure he will be okay. I was the same way. I got sleep. The throwing up didn't really stop, but it will soon, I think. I stub out my cigarette and head back inside. It's freezing.

I see a small red car pull into the drive out front. I can't see who is inside. I wonder if it is the speakers for tonight's AA meeting. I sit down and watch the car through the dining room window. A small, beautiful, brown haired woman gets out of the car. She turns, locks her car door, and walks up to reception.

"There is someone outside," I say. Brian jumps up off the sofa very fast, startling Pat who is also sitting. He beams and runs over to me.

"She's gone to reception," I say smiling. Brian winks and jogs back over through the living room into the reception area. I smile and watch the snow fall outside.

"Oh my *Goooood*!" I hear bellowed from the other room. I laugh hard and look at Abbie.

"He's happy…" I say. Abbie grins and nods, returning to her book she is reading. The door leading from the reception to the living room bursts open and Brian hurries in with his hand grasped onto the woman's hand.

"This is my *gorgeous* wife Jane!" he shouts proudly across the room. His wife smiles nervously and laughs. He brings her over to me and Abbie.

"Jack, love, this is Jane," he says smiling down at me. Jane holds out her hand and I take it.

"Hello," I say.

"Hello, Jack," she says smiling.

"He has not stopped speaking about you, it's lovely to meet you…" I say.

She smiles and kisses Brian's cheek. "Big softie," she says.

He blushes and winks at me. He walks off and introduces Jane to Abbie. I get up and go into the games room. I take the chairs and set them up neatly in a circle. I get a small coffee table and place it in the middle. I head back into the kitchen, get some biscuits and a small plate. I place the biscuits on the coffee table, switch on the light in the room and turn the radiators on.

Tom comes in and smiles.

"Great job, Jack, you looking forward to the meeting tonight?" he says. I shrug.

"I don't believe in God so not so sure how much it can help. I want to try anything though. No point saying no to it at this point."

"You have the right attitude. The God part of it all is subjective. If you don't believe in God, your higher power can be anything," he says.

"Yeah, okay…" I say raising my eyebrows.

"We have about twenty minutes until they arrive so why don't you let everyone know when the meeting is and have a cigarette or something," Tom says, walking out of the room.

I head back out into the living room and tell everyone the meeting is in twenty minutes. Everyone nods their heads and I head outside for a cigarette. Abbie follows me outside with Pat.

I sit on the bench and spark up.

"You been to one of these meetings before?" Abbie asks.

"Yeah, once or twice before I came here. Didn't really help. I don't believe in the higher power thing," I say.

Abbie nods her head. "Me neither."

"It can be anything though, Jack, it doesn't have to be God," Pat says looking sceptically at me.

"If there is a higher power or God, it's a bit strange of me to start believing in it now, when I haven't my entire life. I am the one who picked up, I am the one responsible for it," I say.

Pat looks intent on telling me otherwise. "It is a disease, Jack, addiction," she says.

"I am not saying it isn't. There is definitely something wrong with me inside. Believing that some greater force or God is going to save me from my own actions isn't the answer though. It's me. I am the one to stop myself from drinking. Not God," I say back. I feel passionate about this. "I also appreciate and respect people who believe in it though. I wish I had faith. I really do. But I don't. And I can't change that. Or pretend."

Pat looks at me and smiles.

"Fair enough. It helps me," she says.

"Everybody is different though, aren't they?" I say, smiling back.

Pat nods. Abbie laughs. We sit outside for around ten minutes and I hear a car pulling into the car park. I get up and head into the dining room. I see three people getting out of a car. A woman and two men. The woman is small and has black hair. She is wearing tracksuit bottoms and a hoodie. One man wears glasses and a blazer and smart shirt; the other is very small and also wears a tracksuit.

"They're here," I say to the others. Brian is still in the chill out room with his wife and I don't disturb him. The group head into the games room and I wait outside to greet the visitors.

They come through into reception and I hear them checking in. They come through the doors leading into the main house and I smile at them.

"Hello, I'm Jack, nice to meet you," I say.

"Good to meet you, Jack! I am Sam and this is John and Keith." She motions to the others and I shake their hands.

"Everyone is through there…" I say pointing to the games room.

"Wonderful," Sam says. She walks through the doors, John and Keith follow her.

We all sit down and I point out the biscuits and say they are welcome to them. Sam thanks me and takes one. I ask if they would like a cup of tea or coffee. They say yes and I ask Joe to help me make them. I head out of the room and we go to the kitchen.

On the way through I hear crying coming from the chill out room. It's Brian and he is crying hard. I make the coffees with Joe and we carry them back through to the games room. We give them to the speakers and they thank us.

"Okay, thank you, everyone, for having us today. I am Sam and I am an alcoholic. We are going to say the serenity prayer to start things off. Do any of you know it? If not it is super easy so join in if you like," she says looking around the group. She shuts her eyes, as do Keith and John. Other residents do the same and they start reciting.

"God, grant me the serenity to accept the things I cannot change, the courage to change the things I can, and the wisdom to know the difference."

I don't say it. I kind of know it but I don't speak. I don't shut my eyes. I kind of just want to observe. I don't mind sharing, but the whole thing has always made me pretty uneasy.

"Okay, lovely. So today we will tell you a bit about ourselves. Keith will be sharing his story today, and then we will open the floor up for a discussion. That sound good?" Everyone nods and Sam smiles.

"Great. Well, I am Sam. I am an alcoholic. I have been clean for six years now. I have been in AA the whole time. Thank you very much for having me today," she says.

We all reply, "Hello, Sam," like zombies after she says, 'I am an alcoholic'. They do this in most meetings after someone says the words 'I am an alcoholic'. She proceeds to tell us a little bit about how long she was using for, what her life was like before recovery and how much better things are now. It is inspirational. To be clean for that long is pretty incredible.

John takes over and introduces himself.

"Hello, my name is John and I am an alcoholic…"

"Hello, John…" We all reply.

John was sleeping rough and has been clean for around a year. He now is living in supported accommodation and has got himself a job as a recovery worker. We all congratulate him. He has a baby but has to have no contact with his ex as she has a restraining order against him which makes it difficult. I listen and feel a lot of empathy for him.

Once Sam and John have said a bit about themselves they turn to Keith and invite him to tell his story of recovery and addiction. Keith smiles and moves his chair a little further into the circle.

"Okay, hello, everyone, I am Keith and I am an alcoholic," he says.

"Hello, Keith," we all repeat.

"So I have been using alcohol since I was around nine years old. I had an extremely tough childhood and was physically abused by my dad growing up. When I was younger at home, I didn't want to be there so I ran away a lot, got in with the wrong crowed and Started using within that group."

Everyone is listening, the room is completely silent.

"I hid my drinking from my parents for years. When I was in my late teens I was robbing houses, shops and even my own family. I left home at seventeen as I couldn't stand being around my dad anymore and I moved in with a girl I was seeing. She also like me was an addict. She was addicted to crack and I used to use with her but mainly it was alcohol for me. We robbed to fund our addiction and we didn't care who we hurt. Around this time she became pregnant, and we were terrified. We didn't have enough money to support ourselves let alone a baby. So she decided to have it aborted. I don't think she really wanted to and I felt bad for her, I felt it was my fault. As time went on things got worse within our relationship and I ended up moving out. When I left she had nothing and neither did I. I didn't care. I wanted to leave and I wanted to only take care of myself. I moved in with a friend of mine and then found out a month later she had killed herself."

Keith is visibly very emotional. He isn't crying but his voice is breaking and his eyes are watering.

"After a long time of not looking after myself I tried to get clean. The thought of my ex made me want to do the same. End it all. And I did try countless times. I woke up in hospital over and over again, lost everything and ended up reaching out to the alcohol and drug services," he says.

"With their help I ended up getting clean. I stayed clean for a long time, around seven years. I got myself a job and subsequently met my now long suffering wife of twelve years."

Keith goes quiet for a second, he rubs his face in his hands. He continues. "After a while of being married, work was going well and I hadn't drunk for a long time. We had our beautiful boy Jake after trying years of trying and we were over the moon. Being a dad was a great distraction for a while. I wouldn't have time to think about drinking because I was up night feeding or changing his nappies. I didn't get a lot of sleep at that time and was helping my wife as much as I could. I think it was the lead up to my birthday or something a few years later and I decided to start drinking again. My wife didn't really object, she didn't know the ins and outs of my addictions in the past. I didn't want to tell her and didn't think it was relevant. I was embarrassed about it. I began drinking again and for a long time it was okay. I would drink on weekends, with my wife and our friends at parties and things were okay. I had an accident at work and ended up breaking my leg from a fall off a ladder, which meant I was working from home for a while. I wouldn't do much at home and started slowly turning to drink in the boredom. I started gambling on websites and over the course of a few months things started getting a bit out of control. The pain medication was extremely addictive – which I found out a lot later – and I was taking a lot of them every day with drink. I liked the feeling they gave me and abused it. Soon I spent money we didn't have on the sites I was on. I didn't tell my wife and I acted as though everything was fine. I was taking out loans to keep my head above water and soon had bailiffs knocking on our door. I think it was near the build up to Christmas. I was absolutely skint. My wife had no idea. She came home with a ton of presents for our son and me. She was just doing what we usually do for Christmas but she knew nothing of the trouble we were in. I remember seeing her coming in and my heart just absolutely sinking. I knew we couldn't afford all of this, and I knew she'd used our credit card. I think it was two days before Christmas. I…" He stops and holds his head in his hands.

"Go on, Keith, it's okay," Sam says.

Keith exhales and continues. "My wife had gone to her mum's and taken our son with her to see his grandparents. I was still at home and I didn't know what to do about Christmas. I needed alcohol and had no money. She had our credit card and I didn't have cash. We'd had letters through the door about repossession of property that I had to keep hiding from my wife. I remember it was the night-time and I think they left that day.

"I was panicking and I didn't know what to do. I started withdrawing and I just was freaking out. I took all the presents from under the tree, took off all the wrapping, and put them into the car. I smashed the living room up, kicked in the front door and ransacked our rooms. I tried to make it look like a robbery. I drove the presents which I knew I could sell to a local shop that buys second hand stuff. I sold the lot. I got next to nothing for it all. I went straight to a pub and spent the day drinking. I don't remember leaving the pub and I don't remember getting in the car.

"I didn't stop drinking. I don't know why I did what I did. We needed the money and I thought in my fucked up head this was the right thing to do. I realise now and very soon after that this was the addict in me just making sure I got what I needed. On my drive home I crashed the car. I went straight into a lamppost about a mile from the pub I was at. I broke my collar bone, five ribs, fractured my eye socket. My nose was completely crushed and lost around eight teeth on the steering wheel. I fractured my skull and had a bleed on the brain. I was in a medically induced coma for two days before I came back around."

I see tears on Keith's cheeks.

"I woke up and my wife was by my bedside with my son. She had found out about the debt we were in because I left letters on the side in our destroyed bedroom. She knew I had staged the robbery and she told me she was going to be here for me while I was in hospital, but afterwards if I didn't get help she would leave me. I spent a long time recovering from the accident and eventually I left the hospital. I came back home and the first thing I did was go to an AA meeting in my local village hall. I spoke to the companies I owed money to and I set up payment plans. I sorted my life out. I couldn't lose my wife and my son and I am beyond lucky to have them and AA in my life. I wouldn't be here now without them.

"Anyway, thank you for listening to my share. It means a lot. Thanks."

The room sits in a stunned silence. Everyone looks across at each other.

"We will now open up the room for discussion. Is that okay, Keith?" Sam looks at Keith.

"Sure," he says, nodding his head.

"I thought that was really brave, thank you for sharing," Pat says.

Keith nods his head. "You're welcome."

"Have you found it difficult staying clean for so long?" she asks.

Keith smiles. "Of course. If it was easy there wouldn't be a need for AA or this place. When you realise your life is unmanageable and you don't have a choice, you work as best you can to not lose what you have. My sobriety means I am able to live, be with my family and be happy. There are times when it is difficult, but that is where meetings help so much."

Pat nods her head in agreement.

"Thank you for sharing, Keith, that was difficult to hear and it was brave to tell us that," I say.

Keith smiles appreciatively.

"I am worried because I am young. There are going to be parties and stuff I can't go to anymore. I am worried I won't be contacted by my friends because of it and I'll be alone. I know it sounds silly. I play music and drink was a big part of that at gigs, so I am worried about that too," I say.

"The thing is, Jack, unfortunately there will be people in your life you will have to distance yourself from if they encourage you to use, and these types of people aren't good for your recovery," Sam says.

I nod my head. I know this. Luckily my best friends don't really drink; it's some of the others that this might affect. "Yeah, I know. I have never been too good at meetings though. I never feel like it's helped once I have left. Also I don't believe in a higher power or God, so it's difficult for me to relate to the discussions," I say.

"Yeah, see this is something that a lot of people experience. The thing I've tried to tell people is to pick a word of your choice to replace it. The message of sobriety is the important part. If you can get through to that, religion shouldn't come into it," John says.

I nod my head. I feel like that is an easy answer. I feel angry that there aren't places for people like me. A place where you talk about the struggle of being sober without faith. I would go there. I feel stupid that I can't believe in something greater than myself. I believe in what's in front of me, and science. Not all powerful forces that can't be proven to be true. I don't know. I sit silently and the questions move on around the room. I appreciated Keith's story and I do feel he is inspirational for how far he has come. I haven't had any revelations though.

I feel I have lost interest in the group now. I wish I hadn't but I just don't feel comfortable. The faith and religion part of AA is an elephant in the room for me and now for some reason that's all I can think about.

I sit and listen to the other residents asking their questions. I daydream into the whiteboard and think about other things.

Abbie is speaking to Sam. "I am homeless. So for me not having a home is a huge factor in relapse and always has been for me. I am scared for when I leave here and what happens next."

That would be scary. I can't imagine how that must feel.

"Speak to me after, babe, and I can give you some numbers for places you can contact about supportive housing. I think the staff here is on the case about that for you already though," Sam says.

I look over and Abbie smiles and looks relieved.

"Oh great, that's great thanks," she replies.

The group ends with the serenity prayer again and some of the residents sit and talk to the speakers. I get up. I thank them for coming and head into the living room. Brian comes out of the chill out room with his wife. They are holding hands and look as though they have been crying.

"How was group, love?" Brian asks.

I make an uncomfortable face and shrug. "I didn't get anything from it really. The guy who spoke, his story was interesting though."

"Yeah, they are usually worth a listen," he says, smiling. He and his wife head to the exit.

"Bye, nice to meet you," she says to me.

"You too," I say.

The speakers exit the games room and walk past the door to the living room.

"Bye, Jack, take care." Sam says waving.

"Yeah, you too, bye," I say.

Keith and John follow her and they too head into reception.

Brian comes back out a few minutes later and sits down next to me.

"You okay? You look like you have been crying…" I say.

He smiles and wipes his eyes. "Yeah, im great. My little girl has been a bit sick so I was worried about her, she'll be okay though," he says.

"Yeah, of course she will, mate. Jane seems lovely," I say.

"Right??" he says, grinning again.
I laugh. "You up for a bit of cards tonight?" I ask.
"Course, love, sounds good."

Chapter 23: Psycho

"Hello, Jack, I'm Angie. Do you want to follow me?"

I am sitting watching TV mindlessly when a tall red haired woman enters the living room, smiling at me. I get up.

"Hi, yeah, course, sorry, I was miles away…" I say.

"No problem, let's go into the games room and have a chat," she says.

I follow her into the games room and we sit down opposite each other. Angie is the psychiatrist I was told about. I don't know what to expect but I am glad I am meeting with her.

"So, Jack, how have you been getting on here? You only have a couple of days left I believe?"

She is right. Time has gone fast here. I didn't think it would but it has flown by. Every day at the moment I am feeling lucky to be alive. The thoughts of how I used to be are still there though. I don't want to use again. I feel terror at the thought of it. Suppose that's a good thing.

"Yeah, pretty good. I feel very lucky…"

"I imagine you do," she says, smiling and nodding her head.

I feel awkward. I don't know where to look so I stare at the floor. I feel embarrassed and can't make eye contact. I don't know why.

"I don't know what to talk about..." I say nervously.

"I have gone over your notes. If there is anything in particular you want to discuss we can do that," she says, looking at me with a friendly smile.

"Okay," I reply. "I have been having this dream. I have had it since I was little."

"Okay..." she says.

"I am in a really bright room. There is a massive ball of something, like a massive black mass in the middle of the room..."

She begins writing on a piece of paper.

"What are you writing?" I ask.

"Just taking notes, nothing to worry about," she says.

"Okay. The ball of mass gets more and more aggressive and I feel more and more terrified. I have an impending feeling of doom, like everything is going to end. I feel I can't control the ball of black in the room. It frightens me and I can't move. It makes a noise that scares me, a low grumble, it is menacing..."

Angie nods and frowns.

"...And before I can get the strength to scream or shout or move, it explodes, and I wake up," I say, looking at my hands.

"Okay, that is interesting," she says, again, writing on the paper.

"Really? It's terrifying. The other day in the dream I was drinking. When I drank the alcohol didn't get me drunk. It just hurt and burned. When I woke up, I was sick," I say.

"Has there always been alcohol in the dream?" she asks.

"No."

"Okay…"

She writes some more.

"The drink I assume is because I am getting clean…"

She nods her head and smiles. "Yes, Jack, I agree. It is your subconscious tricking you. It is very common so there is nothing to worry about."

"Okay…"

"This ball of mass in your dream… you say you have had this appear since you were little?"

"Yeah," I say, looking at her, interested. "I only really get it when things are bad, like my anxiety or my drinking etcetera. When I was younger it was very much when my anxiety was present."

She nods. "Yes, okay. How was your relationship with your parents growing up?"

I think. "It was good…" I say. "I mean, yeah, it was good. I only saw my dad on Sundays as my mum and dad are divorced. I didn't have much discipline at home but with my dad, if I did something wrong he would tell me off and I would get anxious about that when I saw him. I didn't want to upset him."

"Okay," she replies.

"I had a great childhood, I think. There were times when things weren't ideal but that is normal. I was a very angry and sensitive kid though. When I was younger I used to not be able to sleep at night because I would worry she or my dad would die, and I would be left alone. I was always really scared of people I love dying. I don't know why, I think that's when my anxiety started…"

"Sure, yeah I can imagine it was tough when your parents divorced," she says.

"Honestly. I don't remember it. It's all I've really known. They were two when they divorced so… I just don't remember it," I say.

She nods her head again and writes on the paper.

"So this ball of mass, and the room you are in. Do you recognise the room?"

"No, it is just a bright white room…"

She nods again. "It seems to me you can't control it. Like the mass is unstable and uncontrollable. Maybe this is a manifestation of your anxiety, fear of death and ongoing addiction. You can't control these parts of your life. This in turn terrifies you. It is an unstable phobia," she says.

"Fuck, yeah maybe," I say. I sit in silence and think. That does make a lot of sense. I don't know. "The other day when I woke up I felt dizzy and sick, does that mean anything? I thought there was something really wrong with me…"

"If, in the dream, what you were doing made you feel sick, then you can in turn feel sick when you wake up."

"Yeah, that makes sense," I say.

We sit in silence for a minute or two. I think she is right about the dream.

"Is there anything I can do about the nightmare?" I say.

"Well. All we can do is try and work on your anxiety and maybe in turn this will help to stop it," she says.

"Yeah, yeah, okay."

Angie looks at her piece of paper. The paper is sitting in a folder and I see a picture of me poking out of the top of it. I look dreadful. To be fair I don't look much better now, but I looked especially bad then.

"Why do the files have a photo of us in them?" I ask.

"Just to put a face to the name, also for you to look at when your treatment is done, remind you how far you have come."

"Okay," I say. "If I am honest, I have seen therapists and counsellors before. Growing up I was always a bit nuts. My mum tried her best to help me find out what was wrong, but we never got anywhere with it."

"Nuts how?" she says.

"I would lose my temper all the time. I fought a lot with kids in school and had horrible thoughts."

"What type of thoughts?" she says.

"Thoughts of killing myself, hurting others, opening car doors while I'm traveling in them. The list goes on and on. I never actually wanted to hurt anyone or do these things, but the thoughts would pop into my head and it would make me feel like I am mad," I say, I am back to looking at my hands again.

"What age did you start having these thoughts?" she asks.

"Around five years old."

"You can remember that far back?"

"Yes. I can remember very far back. I don't know why."

She looks at me. I don't know what she is thinking and this makes me nervous. I want to know. I want to know if she thinks I'm fucking mental. I want to know if afterwards she is going to report me to the staff, for having disturbing thoughts.

"I still worry about things. I don't know whether I am all there in my head…"

She keeps her gaze on me.

"You're not mad, Jack. In fact I would say you are an intelligent, caring person. From what I was told you were extremely determined to get better," she says.

"I was. I am."

"I know. What it sounds like is that you have been experiencing intrusive thoughts. This can be associated with OCD; Borderline personality disorder can also be a possibility," she says.

"I've never even been told about those disorders. I've heard of OCD but not the other one," I say.

"People with BPD tend to think in extremes. It is something called 'dichotomous'. Some people call it by other names but for you this feels like the case. Thinking about death, fixating on doom and dread. Thinking the worst or even the best in situations and not much in-between."

"Yeah, that sounds about right," I say. I do all of those things. I don't know why it has taken this long to speak to someone who can shed a bit of light on my fucked up brain. "I don't really feel it's OCD though."

"Well we will know more once we do a full assessment. We can't do this here but once you leave we can set up outpatient appointments."

"Okay, yeah, please," I say. "So then I'm not a psycho? I was scared I might be."

"No, you're certainly not. Psychos don't have signs of empathy and you clearly have a lot of that. Why would you worry about your mum and dad not being here if you were a psychopath?" she says smiling.

"Yeah, true. I don't know, I guess because it's been left for so long I just thought I was the only one who felt these things and that I was going mad," I say.

"Well I can say with absolute certainty you are not, Jack," she says. She looks down at her file and looks back at me. "You say you have had thoughts of killing yourself."

"Yeah, I do think that a lot. Mostly when I am drinking to be honest," I say.

"And have you ever tried?" she says.

"I don't know, not really. I have cut myself up pretty bad before, but I guess I have always been too much of a coward to go through with it properly."

"Jack, that doesn't make you a coward. I will get in touch with some places that can help with how you are feeling when you leave. I will also be putting you forward for CBT," she says flicking through her file.

"What is that?" I say confused.

"CBT is cognitive behavioural therapy. It is a great way to try and change your mind set and it helps with the things you are experiencing. I feel it will do you a world of good."

"Right. Okay," I say back.

Angie closes the file and looks back at me.

"Well, Jack, I will do all I can on my end to get you the help, finally," she says. She stands and I do the same. She takes my hand and shakes it. "I really do wish you all the best on a successful recovery and hope things improve mentally, with my help, they will I hope." She smiles.

"Thank you, really it means a lot. It was very nice to meet you," I say back.

"You too," she says.

She turns and heads out of the games room and is gone. I feel slightly better, like I have a fighting chance at sorting myself out now. Hopefully this is going to help me stay on the right track and be a better, normal person.

Chapter 24: A little trip

I wake up and the sun is streaming through my window. I leave the day after tomorrow. The time has flown by. I am very anxious about leaving. The trials I have faced so far are nothing compared to the outside world.

I feel strong. So much stronger than when I came in here. I am eating well, sleeping and no longer being sick. I generally don't feel like I am going to die. I forgot what a good feeling that could be. I sit up and look out of my window. The sun is melting the last bits of snow on the tree branches, and birds flit to and fro. I turn to my whiteboard and see the same writing I have seen every day. It's funny how such a simple thing as this can grant so much strength to me. I have looked at these words at my darkest times and it has helped me so much.

I throw on some clothes and exit my room. I knock on each of the residents' doors one by one, telling them that it's time to get up. Today is Brian's last day. He is being picked up by his wife tonight and hasn't stopped talking about it.

I am happy for him.

I head over to the medical room and knock.

Dev answers. "Morning, Jack."

"Morning, bud," I say. I sit down on the usual chair and wait as he gets my medication ready.

"Not long now for you, is it?" he says, smiling down at me.

"Yeah," I say smiling. "Bit nervous about leaving…"

"You have done so well, mate. I am sure you will smash it out there," he says. He passes me my medication, Which by now is nothing more than a few vitamins and a very small amount of Librium.

I take the tablets, drink some water and pass the empty cup to Dev.

"Brian's leaving today isn't he?" I say.

"Yep! I hope he cracks it this time…" he says.

I hear uncertainty in Dev's voice. I guess because Brian has been here before, he is sceptical.

"I reckon he will do okay."

"Let's hope so, mate, let's hope so," he says.

I get up and thank Dev. I leave the room and head down the corridor.

I see Sid coming out of his room.

"How we doing, mate?" I say.

Sid smiles and nods. "Yeah, getting there," He says.

"You get some sleep last night?" I ask.

He nods again. "Yeah, a couple of hours."

"That's better than nothing, man!" I say, smiling. He smiles back and I head downstairs.

It is quiet and no one is around. I clear up some bits from the dining table, some cups and small plates. I take them into the kitchen and clean them. I switch on the kettle and head back into the living room and sit down. I open my journal and look over some of the pages from my first days here. It is very surreal and crazy to see how I was then and how I am now. I am scared still but for completely different reasons. I know I can't drink again. I know my body can't take it. I will end up exactly how I was before I came in here, and I can't go through that again. Sid enters the living room and sits down.

"Kettle's on," I say. Sid looks up, looking tired. "You want a coffee, buddy?"

"A tea would be great," he says.

I smile and get up. I head into the kitchen, make Sid a cup of tea and a coffee for myself. I head back to him and hand over his tea.

"Thank you," he says.

"Not a problem," I say smiling.

Sid raises the cup to his mouth and his hands shake violently. Tea falls onto his jumper.

"Little tip, mate, try using both hands, your shakes are pretty bad still," I say smiling.

He smiles back and holds the cup with both hands which steadies it. "Thanks, Jack."

"No worries. Don't worry, mate, that will go with time, it's a pain in the arse I know," I say.

The colour in his face isn't there yet. Still pale with yellow eyes. He is stick thin. He told us he lives on the streets and was very lucky to get help. I really feel for him. He has no family and is all alone. I can't even begin to fathom how difficult that must be. I have a huge amount of respect for him.

He has been given some clean clothes by the staff and they hangs off him. When his appetite comes back he will be in heaven. The food here is pretty amazing. The past couple of days he hasn't eaten hardly anything. Same as me when I got here. You eat, you throw up, you get no sleep and the pattern continues. Until one day it starts to get easier. He is still in the early stages of treatment, so he won't get much rest yet.

Tom comes into the living room and approaches Sid.

"Hello, Sid, how you doing this morning?"

"Pretty shit," he replies.

"Don't worry, you'll feel better soon. I just wanted to let you know that we have been in touch with somewhere that can give you after care when you leave here. It is a rehab facility relatively close by. They are just speaking to your care worker to sort out the details," Tom says.

Sid looks like he might cry.

"I don't know what to say… Thank you, mate, really, thank you."

Sid begins to cry. His hands reach up to wipe off tears and he shakes violently.

"No problem, Sid, it's going to be all right. You received your meds this morning?" Tom says.

"Yeah," Sid responds. "Really… thank you…" He wipes his eyes and smiles at Tom.

"No problem, see you in a bit."

Tom walks out. I look at Sid.

"See, mate! Things are looking up already," I say.

He smiles back and nods. He wipes his eyes again and with both hands, lifts his mug and drinks.

I roll a cigarette and head outside. The ground and trees are covered with melted snow. I sit on the bench and smoke. I can see Brian entering the living room. He looks like he is dancing. I can see a very big smile on his face. He turns around and seems to be speaking to Sid. Brian waves his arms up and down. I hear raised voices but can't tell if it is because of an argument or whether Brian is just being loud. I walk back inside.

"Don't talk to me like that, you little bitch!"

"You are too fucking loud! I am not feeling well and you are too much right now!"

Brian is standing over Sid. Sid is looking up at Brian, apprehensively. Brian is a nice guy but I have seen him lose his temper once before and I know he can be quite intimidating.

"I've been here longer than you so shut your fucking mouth!" Brian shouts loudly at Sid.

"Brian!" I shout across the room. "Pack it in, he isn't feeling well. Just leave him alone!"

Brian turns around. His cheeks are flushed and he looks hurt. "Oh, you want me to shut up as well now, rock star?" he says. I can tell he is semi joking but I can see Sid is scared.

"No, mate, but he has just got here, remember how you felt when you first arrived? Leave him the fuck alone," I say, raising my voice and standing up.

Brian stands where he is. He rolls his eyes at me and turns back to Sid. "Just don't tell me what to fucking do, okay, love?"

"Don't call me love. I wasn't trying to start anything I was just asking—"

"Yeah, yeah, whatever, love." Brian walks towards me and bumps his shoulder into mine. I smile and laugh.

"Calm down, you tit," I say.

Brian laughs, throws his hand in the air and disappears into the kitchen. I walk over to Sid and sit next to him.

"Sorry, mate, you okay?" I say.

Sid has his hand on his forehead and looks anxious.

"I wanted to floor that prick. All I said was can you keep it down, he walked in singing and dancing…"

"Yeah, he likes to do that," I say. "Don't worry, mate, he is a big softie really."

"Right… whatever." Sid says, keeping his eyes on the TV.

"Let me know if you need anything, okay?" I say, standing up and walking out the room.

"Yeah. Sure," I hear sarcastically behind me.

Good start to the day. Fuck me.

I don't know why but I feel slightly manic today. Everything is causing me anxiety and I feel I am always on the edge of a panic attack. I go up to my room and I open my journal. I write inside about how I am feeling. I think this is because I know I am leaving soon and I won't have the constant care on the outside that I have in here. I don't know. I know it is a silly thing to worry about but it makes me feel panicked. I am still having the strange dreams. So vivid and terrifying. I am told this will pass and things will get easier in that regard but it still isn't nice to experience.

I have an appointment at the hospital today. Dev asked us all yesterday if we would like to get tested for STIs and I said yes. I haven't had any symptoms or anything but I have had a lot of unprotected sex when I have been drunk so it is a good idea. I also have a liver function test to do. I think they are just taking blood for that so shouldn't be there long.

I go and have a shower, shave and get dressed. Most of the house is up now and I can hear people milling about the corridor. I put on some shoes and head out of my room. Dev comes out of the medical room.

"Ready?"

"Yup," I say.

I follow him down to the entrance and go out the front doors. We get in the car and drive out of the car park. I feel awkward. I don't know why. Car journeys are difficult with people I don't know as I feel I need to fill the silence by talking.

"So how long have you been at the detox centre?" I ask.

"A couple of years now. I have a family member who is an addict so it feels good to do something to help," he says.

"Yeah, I can imagine it's really rewarding…"

"It is. I do see a lot of things which are quite upsetting but that kind of comes with the territory."

I nod. I saw one patient with delirium tremens and it terrified me. I can't imagine the things he has seen, I don't really want to either. I think about asking who in his family is an addict but decide not to as this could be a personal question. We drive through some back roads and into the town centre. I haven't been here before even though I don't live too far away. Everything is very grey and depressing. There is a river that runs through the town and boats are moored along it. I see families walking along the pavements; homeless people huddled in a doorway of a closed down shop and a musician busking in a busy side street.

I used to busk myself. I stopped doing it a while ago. Me and Isaac would skip school and get a bus down to Brighton with my guitar and a harmonica. We would set up in the north lanes, outside a shop called Loot and spend the day playing to shoppers passing by. Thinking about this now makes me smile and I remember it so fondly. We would make quite a bit of money, head up to a coffee shop near the bus stop afterwards and sit people watching until our bus home arrived. I miss doing that.

We pull into the car park of the hospital and Dev switches off the engine.

"Ready, bud?" he says looking at me and smiling.

"Yeah," I say.

We get out and head towards the entrance. This hospital isn't as nice as the one near my house. The walls are grey and it doesn't look like it has been renovated since it was built. We walk into the reception area and approach the counter.

"Hello, appointment for Jack Mackey?" Dev says to the woman at the desk. She keeps her eyes on the computer screen.

"One moment," she replies.

Dev turns to me and smiles and I wait. It feels very odd to be in a hospital and not be withdrawing. I look around and see people sitting in the A and E waiting area. It is quite full. I remember sitting with my mum, on so many occasions, waiting to be fixed whilst hallucinating and shaking. I feel so fucking grateful right now.

"Okay, if you would like to go down the corridor, take the lift up to the third floor and turn right," the woman behind the desk says to Dev. He looks over at me and I raise my eyebrows and follow.

We reach the third floor and Dev tells me to wait on some chairs near another desk and I do so. I take in my surroundings. Usually even on a different floor of a hospital it's still pretty busy, but up here it's a ghost town.

Dev comes over with a nurse following.

"Okay, Mr. Mackey if you would like to follow me." She smiles and I stand up.

"Good luck, mate," Dev says, winking.

"Yeah… thanks," I say. I have a horrible feeling, I know what's coming. I follow her down a bright corridor and into a small room. She instructs me to sit on a chair and I do so.

"So, Jack, what we will be doing is an STI test, this will involve us taking some bloods and also a swab," she says.

"Where is the swab going, can I ask?" I say, knowing full well what's coming.

She smiles awkwardly. I go red. She laughs.

"This is a very normal procedure, Jack, there is no need to worry," she says smiling.

"Okay, never had anything like that done," I say, also smiling.

"Don't worry, won't take a couple of minutes."

I follow her into a clean white room and she proceeds to take a swab for the test. I don't know what to do or where to look. I stare at the ceiling.

"I am told you are in the detox facility nearby," she says, turning her back and putting the swab into a clear tube.

"I am, finally. Very lucky…" I say.

She turns and looks at me. She smiles. "I bet," she says. "So we will send the results to the facility, you will get those before you leave to go home."

"Great," I say.

"If you wait here, someone will be in to take your blood in a few minutes."

"Okay," I say.

She exits the room and I sit and stare into the ceiling again. I feel good I am having this all checked. My liver needs to be looked at, and I am very nervous about what to expect. I think about my friends. I wonder what they are up to. I wonder whether I am missing out on anything. Suppose if I were at home I wouldn't be well enough to see them anyway. I think about my family, wonder what they are doing. I wonder what it feels like to not have this happening. To wake up and start the day knowing that I can do anything. No addiction, endless possibilities. Fuck.

I need to not think like that. It's negative and the reason I am fucking here. I *can* do anything now because I am *not* drinking.

I know now that I can't. Every single fucking time I think I am okay to do it again I end up back where I started. Madness is doing the same thing over and over again and expecting different results, I am not mad, not anymore at least.

Another nurse enters the room.

"How we doing?"

"Yeah, not too bad," I say smiling.

She heads over to me. "Can you roll up your sleeve for me, Jack?"

"Sure."

She places a strap around my bicep and clicks on a small machine next to her. It inflates around my arm, getting tighter and more uncomfortable, and then deflates.

"Your blood pressure is looking good."

"Awesome," I say.

"Do you mind needles?" she asks.

"Nope, not at all," I say.

She proceeds to insert the needle into my arm and drains it of blood into three clear tubes.

"Okay, Jack, so what we will do is check the functionality of your liver and if there is anything abnormal we will let you know, either way we will contact you," she says.

"Okay, sounds good."

She smiles. I stand.

"Thank you," I say.

"No problem, you take care," she says.

I leave and meet back up with Dev.

"All good?" he says.

"Yup, sweet," I say.

We walk back down to the car and I stop before getting in to have a cigarette.

"Sorry, man," I say.

"Take your time."

"Thank you for taking me today."

"My pleasure!" he says, smiling.

I smile back. I smoke the cigarette quickly and we get into the car. I rest my head against the window and shut my eyes. I feel a bit sick. Slightly dizzy. I haven't really been out since I arrived at detox and my anxiety is flaring up a bit. I shut my eyes and try to calm myself. Everything is fine. If I were this way before I would think it was withdrawal. It can't be, not anymore, just normal, plain anxiety. Still feels horrible.

We pass back through the grey town until we reach the countryside. The green blur of trees whipping past the window makes me feel sick. I shut my eyes and slow my breathing.

"You okay, mate?" Dev asks.

"Yeah, fine, man, Just feel anxious and a bit sick."

"No worries, mate, let me know if you want to pull over. We will be back momentarily anyway," he says.

We pull back down the country lane towards the facility. I immediately start to feel better when I can see the front door. I guess it is the fear of being stuck in the car, breathing out of control and feeling trapped. We drive into the car park and my breathing slows.

Chapter 25: Goodbye Brian

"You excited?"

"Yes, love, very."

Brian is packing his clothes into a large suitcase in his room, I am in the doorway. It kind of smells in here, of B.O. and stale aftershave. It feels weird to say, but I will miss him. He was a source of comedy and happiness when I felt upset and scared here. His family will be here in about half an hour and I can tell he is nervous.

"Okay, man, well I will leave you to it..." I say.

He looks over and smiles. "Okay, love, in a bit."

I head downstairs and everyone is lounging around the living room. Sid, again, is sitting on the sofa looking pale.

"All right, Sid?" I ask.

He looks up at me and forces a smile, he nods. I smile back and head outside. It feels strange to know I will be gone tomorrow night. The anticipation of it makes my heart skip a beat. I sit down and think for a while. About the long and terrifying journey I have been on. I am proud of myself, for accomplishing something that I didn't think I had in me.

"Can I have a word, Jack?"

Tom has poked his head out of the back door of the garden and is calling me in.

"Sure," I say.

I get up and walk inside. I follow Tom into the games room where three chairs are arranged together in front of me.

"Have a seat, buddy."

I sit down and Lynne enters the room. She and Tom take their seats. Tom is handed a thick file and flicks through it. A picture of me, taken when I came in, flashes past in the sea of pages. The memory of that day also flashes in my mind. How terrified and anxious I was. How sad and devastated I felt to not have my mum there.

"So... Jack..." Tom says, looking at me and smiling. "How are you feeling?"

I look at him and Lynne quizzically. "Err, yeah, I'm feeling okay I think," I say.

They both smile.

"We just wanted to get you in here to talk about your stay with us and the next steps when you leave," Tom says, again, looking at the file.

"Okay," I say.

"I think it's safe to say you have done brilliantly, Jack," Tom says, looking at Lynne, smiling. "You have been very focused and I can see how much this means to you."

"Yes, well, I would be dead if I didn't come here. You guys have saved my life," I say, starting to feel a lump in my throat.

They both smile empathetically.

"It's true we gave you the chance to get clean and sober, Jack, but the real work has come from you. You have to want to stay sober, you have to want to live and be determined to give up what was making you so ill. That is exactly what you have done and you should be so proud of yourself. Myself and Lynne have seen you getting up early to wake people up for meds. We have seen the effort you go to, to check if people are okay. The way you set up the room for meetings, setting out biscuits and drinks, is really something. You should be proud, Jack."

I feel myself going red. "Thanks, Tom, Thanks, Lynne. I just don't want to let my family down," I say.

"Yes, but more importantly, Jack, don't let *yourself* down," Lynne responds.

I nod. "Yeah, you're right."

"So when you leave us tomorrow, I assume you will be returning to your mum's?" Tom says.

"Yeah, I will," I say.

"I bet she is excited to see you," Lynne says.

"Yeah, maybe," I say grinning. "She is probably pretty nervous too."

"Well, you can understand why she would be though," Tom says.

"Of course," I say.

"I just want to say, Jack..." Lynne speaks. She is looking at me intently.

"Yes?" I say.

"I can honestly say it has been such a pleasure to have you here. I don't want you to come back, in the nicest sense, but it has been a real joy to have met you. I have faith in you and I think that you will do well when you leave here. Obviously there are going to be challenges, but you know that. You still have some work to do on yourself, but again, you know that."

"Thanks, Lynne, that really means the world. I know I have a ton of work to do on myself but I feel I can finally start on that. I honestly don't know what I would've done without all of your help. Thank you, from the bottom of my heart, it's changed my life," I respond.

They both smile.

"I echo what Lynne just said. I don't want you fucking back here, Jack, Okay? Your family are so happy you are better, let's not let them down eh?" Tom says.

I smile. Tom has a real hard, tough love exterior and personality. He quite often in groups has taken no shit. He can spot a faker, someone trying to play the key workers and doesn't sugar coat the truth. I love this about him and it is something I find weirdly comforting. If I am not doing well, he would fucking tell me. Before coming here I had been told about him. Not anything about his life or anything personal but a lot about his tough love approach to helping addicts.

"Thanks, Tom, in the nicest possible way, I really don't want to come back here either," I say. I smile. They smile. I stand up. I shake Tom's hand and then Lynne's.

"Well done, buddy, keep up the good work," Tom says, patting me on the shoulder.

"Thanks."

I walk out onto the landing and see a beautiful woman, with brown hair and a baby strapped to her front, coming through the front door of the reception. This must be Brian's wife. It doesn't surprise me that he is with a beautiful woman. He isn't your stereotypical attractive man. He is overweight with red blotches on his face and a receding hairline, but his personality is fantastic. He is loud and outrageous, but also warm and caring.

I smile and walk up the stairs towards the bedrooms.

I approach Brian's door and knock. I can hear heavy breathing coming from inside.

"Brian?" I say.

I hear shuffling and the door opens.

"Your family is here, buddy," I say.

"Thanks, love. I'm really panicking," he says.

"Why?"

"I don't know, I'm scared I will let them down again. I feel safe here and I am scared to leave," he says. He is fidgeting and looks anxious.

"Brian, mate, you will be fine. You are a good person and I have no doubt that you will be fine. Have a little faith in yourself, mate."

Brian comes over and hugs me. It is a very tight hug. Like being hugged by a bear.

"Thanks, Jack."

"No problem. Come on, your wife and baby are downstairs," I say.

His eyes light up and he packs his last remaining bits and follows me out of the room. As we walk he knocks on doors and says a quick goodbye to the other residents still in their rooms.

We get to the top of the stairs and Brian overtakes me in a hurry. I stay standing where I am and I hear him greeting his wife. He doesn't need me there getting in the way. I smile and I feel made up for him. I hear them both sobbing and hugging. I hear Brian talking to his baby, doing funny voices and laughing hysterically.

Brian says goodbye to Tom and thanks him for all his help. I hear Tom tell him to stay safe and to not come back. Brian agrees with Tom and his wife says she will keep him safe.

Brian appears at the bottom of the stairs and startles me.

"Not going to say goodbye, rockstar?" he says, looking up at me.

"Sorry, mate, yeah course," I say. I come down the stairs and I embrace him once again.

"Stay positive, keep safe and remember why you want to be clean, buddy," I say, barely able to get the words out he is hugging me so tight.

"Thanks, love, I will try my best," he replies.

He lets me go and walks back into the entrance where his wife is waiting. I hear them say thank you again and the door opening. The door closes and they are gone.

Good luck, Brian. Good to meet you.

Chapter 26: Black mass

I'm in a bright room.

In front of me is a ball of black mass, contorting and vibrating. I try to approach the ball of darkness and it juts violently, growing larger for a split second. I step away. The more I watch it, the more I can see it growing. It's close to me. Its surface is rough and violent, like the surface of a black sun.

I can feel a heat coming from it. The warmth hits me and it doesn't burn me, instead I feel a searing pain inside my chest. The pain is so bad that I want to die. I scream out. My voice is muffled and I can't hear myself. I wrap my arms around my head and collapse into a ball on the floor. I scream louder. Nothing. Just the humming from the black mass.

I grip my chest with my hands and claw at it. I want this pain to stop. I scream. Nothing. Silence.

I wake up and again, I am soaked in sweat. I am holding my chest and breathing rapidly. My mouth is dry and my clothes feel damp. I think I pissed myself.

It's evening now and it is quiet. My room is dark with a stream of light from the streetlamp outside my window, illuminating the room in an orange glow. I get up. Fuck.

I thought I was past feeling like this. I thought I wouldn't have that dream anymore.

I get up and I pull my trousers off. Grab my towel and head out into the hallway towards the shower room.

It's empty. I enter and remove the rest of my clothes.

I twist the tap and wait for the water to get warm. I stand underneath it and close my eyes. I imagine the water is something different. A magic liquid that can wash away my anxiety and stress. I am starting to feel more calm now. I wash myself, step out and dry myself off. I look in the mirror. I look tired, but apart from that, the colour in my face is returning and I am looking better than I ever have recently.

I can smell food downstairs. I go to my room, change into some jogging bottoms and a jumper. I pull off the wet bed sheets and bundle them up in my arms with some other washing.

Everybody is in the front room downstairs. I walk past them and go to the washing machine. I put in my clothes and switch it on.

"First time I've seen you use that, you dirty fucker!"

I laugh. Tom is stood behind me in the entrance to the utility room.

"Yeah, it hasn't been on my mind until now. I had a small accident. Pissed the bed." I feel myself going red. It's so embarrassing saying it out loud.

"Oh, no worries at all, Jack, I will get someone to put more sheets in your room and change the mattress. Don't worry about it at all," Tom says.

"I'm pretty worried actually. I haven't had a problem with that since coming here. I had a bad 'using' dream and I woke up soaked," I say.

"It is perfectly normal, Jack, remember that up until recently you were abusing your body massively. There are going to be some bumps in the road you're on now but it'll be okay, don't worry and don't feel bad about it."

I smile.

"Thanks, Tom."

"No problem. Now are you coming to group after dinner? It's your last one before you leave tomorrow! Think it'll be very beneficial," he says.

"Sure, I'll be there."

Tom nods and walks out. I head into the kitchen and make myself a coffee.

The smell of cooked beef and pasta floats through the doorway. My stomach lurches and my mouth waters. One thing I will miss about this place is the food. Jesus, the food is good. Getting my appetite back is one of the best things to happen since getting sober. I honestly never thought I would be able to eat again. I am starting to actually look forward to dinner now, something that hasn't happened in years.

I stir my coffee and chuck the spoon into the sink. I drink a quarter of it fast and burn my mouth slightly, but the burning in my stomach feels good.

"Dinner, guys," I hear Mel say. I hear people shuffling into the dining room and I follow. Laid out on the table is lasagne, a large plate of beef and vegetables. It looks incredible. I sit down next to Joe.

"Your last meal, mate," he says, smiling.

"I know, man, feels very weird," I say back. "It's gone so fast, going to miss this place, a bit nervous about going home…"

"Don't be, man, I know it's scary and I can understand that, but it'll be okay. Just keep on staying strong and you'll be fine," he says.

I smile and lean over to the plate of lasagne. I scoop up a large portion and dump it down onto my plate. It really does smell amazing. I serve myself up some vegetables and eat. I look around and everyone is talking to each other. Tom has joined us for dinner. He usually does and I think it shows that he really cares. He usually asks everyone how they are doing and catches up on anything he may have missed throughout the day.

"So when are you off?" I ask Joe.

"Not until next week. They are trying to sort out a place for me to go afterwards. I'm not allowed back to my mum's," he says, between mouthfuls.

I don't want to pry too much. "Ah nice, man, I hear they sorted Sid out so I'm sure it'll be sweet."

He nods. "So it's Jack's Last night!" Joe says over the talking.

I smile.

"You looking forward to getting back home, buddy?" he says.

"Yup, bit nervous though."

"It'll be okay, Jack." Abbie says smiling at me.

"Yeah, it's natural to be nervous, Jack, but you'll be okay," Tom says. "Just keep up the good work out there, okay?"

"Sure, I will," I say. Thoughts of being in situations with drink flash in my mind. It is scary. I don't know what to really expect when I leave. I have never experienced anything like this place before. The tools I have learned here have been valuable but genuinely I think the terror of what I have experienced when withdrawing will keep me on the right path.

I look over at Sid and he is looking tons better. He is eating, which is important and I know that first hand. He looks over at me and I smile, he smiles back. I get up, take my plate and place it at the end of the table with the others. I feel full and sleepy, but it's a good feeling.

I head outside and spark up a cigarette. Tom follows me out.

"Jack, I wanted to have a word," he says. He sits down next to me and looks serious.

"Sure, what's up?" I say.

"Paul passed away last night."

"What? How? I mean, how did that happen?" I say. I don't understand. He was standing in front of me a few days ago. What the fuck.

"Unfortunately, his liver was in a very bad way. I think the heart attack may have been linked to the severe withdrawal you witnessed. Honestly they haven't told me much but I will be getting more information soon. I just thought you should know. I don't want to announce it to everyone," he says. He has a very concerned look on his face.

"Fuck," I say. I feel angry. I feel angry at the fact that if he knew alcohol could do that to him would he have started drinking. I feel angry that not more people know alcohol does this. I feel fucking angry.

"I'm going to go inside and set up for the meeting. Are you okay?" Tom says, patting me on the back.

"Yeah. I'll be in soon."

Tom walks away and I sit. I feel sick. I feel like I should've got to know him, looked after him, checked on him. Maybe if I checked on him he could've got help sooner. Fuck. He was here literally the other day. I have never really known anyone who's died. I didn't really know him but he was like me. He was an addict. This is the reality of addiction. This is fucking terrifying. Why the fuck is this not common knowledge? Why can't more people know about this?

I head back inside. I don't want to go to group but I know I have to. Abbie comes over.

"Just heard about Paul…"

"Yeah, me too, I feel sick," I say.

"I can't hug you, because of the rules, but I would if I could," she says, smiling. I smile back.

"Thanks, Abbie, that means a lot. I feel guilty and I don't know why."

"Jack, you have nothing to feel guilty about, this is something that happens unfortunately. There is nothing any of us could've done," she says.

"Okay," I say. I smile at her again and she motions to the games room.

"Group?"

"Yeah, sure," I say.

I follow Abby. Everyone is sitting in a circle. Tom is running tonight's group and he is busy writing on the whiteboard. I sit down in an empty seat.

"Okay, guys, tonight I thought we could talk about triggers. Triggers are the things in your life that make you feel the urge to drink. It can be anything, everyone is different. As it's Jack's last night here I thought this would be an important one, as when he leaves here, there will be triggers that he will have to face."

Everyone looks at me.

"Okay, cool," I say smiling.

"So, Jack, let's start with you, what do you feel triggers your cravings?" Tom says, holding a marker up to the whiteboard in preparation for my answer.

"I don't know, um, I have friends that I drink a lot with, maybe that?"

Tom writes 'FRIENDS' up on the board.

"Good, Jack, good start."

"Also I guess mental health? Depression?" I say. Others in the room all nod and some mutter in agreement.

"Absolutely, Jack. These are both very, very common triggers. Addicts tend to self-medicate with their drug of choice. It is an escape and the feeling of euphoria can take those feelings away for a short time. Unfortunately we all know that feeling is very short lived," Tom says. He writes 'MENTAL HEALTH' on the board.

I start to think about the friends I drink with. I start wondering whether they will want to see me if I am not drinking. I guess if they do want to stick around, then they are real friends. If not, then I will know who is in my life for the right reasons.

"Environment?" Pat says in a hushed, soft voice. I feel like I haven't heard Pat say a word since I accidentally walked in on her in the shower room. I haven't really tried to make conversation because I feel mortified about it.

"Good one, Pat!" Tom says, writing her suggestion on the whiteboard.

"I don't really have anyone else with me at home, I would just drink to feel less alone in my house," Pat says.

"I was the same," Sarah says. Sarah is in her late twenties and someone who I really haven't spoken to since being here. She has long brown hair, tied tightly in a bun on the top of her head. She wears glasses and is always wearing a different colour variation of the same looking tracksuit every day. My feeling is that she isn't here to make friends and I can understand that. To be fair it isn't the best place to make friends at all, so I just assumed she wants to just get better. Either that or she just doesn't like anyone but Abbie, I'm not entirely sure.

"I'm sure everyone here will relate to these. In a way that's a good thing, it shows the mutual struggle you all have, which in turn lets you know you aren't alone in this," Tom says. "The word environment can relate to so many things in addiction. Maybe you and your friends all meet up every night at the same pub. Maybe your living situation is difficult, in which case drink and drugs can feel like the escape you need. It doesn't have to be that way. What I want to get across to you all, is that we here at Bridge House detox your body. Detoxing your mind is the next step. Triggers are things that make you feel compelled to drink or use drugs. Understanding and recognising those triggers will aid your recovery tenfold, but they may always be there."

Sarah nods; we all nod.

"Smells?" Joe adds. He laughs as he says it and I laugh too.

"Not a common one! Still though, if you feel that may be a trigger Joe, then it goes on the board," Tom says smiling at Joe and Craig who are laughing together. Tom turns and writes 'SMELLS' on the white board.

"What about music?" Abbie says. "Sometimes when I hear music it reminds me of going out and getting fucked, that can be a trigger, can't it?" she says.

"Absolutely. That is another one not many people think about. It can literally be anything though; this is what I am trying to say. It's your perception of a trigger that is important to understand. So for example, what may give you those thoughts and feelings, won't necessarily affect Jack in the same way because his triggers are linked to his own personal memories, feelings and environment. The important part of this group is that it's making you think about them, so you can recognise them and know when it is a trigger."

I know Tom wanted this group to be helpful to me and it kind of is, but it is also making me realise how much my life is going to change when I leave. I feel a bit overwhelmed and like I want to run and hide. I can feel sweat forming on the back of my neck. I feel claustrophobic and hot.

"Can I go get some air, Tom?" I ask.

Everyone looks round and Tom looks confused.

"We will be done in a bit, Jack, this group is important for you?"

"I know, sorry, I'm just not feeling great."

"Okay, we will be out soon," Tom says.

I stand up and rush towards the door. I enter the living room and I sit down breathing heavily. I feel awful, I feel sick and like I can't breathe, my chest feels tight.

"Jack? Everything okay?"

Mel walks in and approaches me looking concerned.

"I feel like I'm having a heart attack…"

She comes over and puts a hand on my back.

"Just try to breathe slowly, Jack, everything will be okay."

I feel panicked and I can't think straight.

"I'll be back in a minute, Jack, stay here," Mel says.

She walks off into the kitchen and I sit in silence on the sofa. All I can hear is my own breath and it's making me feel worse. I shut my eyes and my head spins. I feel like all the blood's gone from my face.

Mel reappears with a cup of something.

"Here, drink this…"

She passes me the mug. It's hot and it smells very strange.

"What is it?" I ask. I put the mug down as I have started shaking.

"It's relaxation tea. It tastes awful, but it really helps with anxiety! Give it a go, I promise it'll help."

She smiles down at me and I feel slightly better.

"Okay," I say. I pick up the mug of tea and I drink. Fuck me, she was not wrong. It tastes like plants and dirt.

She notices my expression and laughs. "Told you! Trust me it really helps," she says.

"Thank you, Mel. I really appreciate it," I say. I drink more. The warm drink is helping me calm down slightly. I breathe slowly and calm myself.

"No problem, just let me know if you want any more. I've seen a lot of people come through this place with terrible anxiety and this has always helped."

Mel walks away into the office and I stay sitting. My head feels like it's clearing already. Maybe it's being told the drink will help, either way I don't care, I'm starting to feel better. I put the mug down, roll a cigarette and go outside. I still can't believe it's my last night. It's gone so fast and I kind of don't want to leave. I really feel safe here.

I see the others leave the games room and file out into the living room. Tom comes out too and spots me outside. He walks through the living room and makes his way out to me. He comes over and sits next to me.

"Feeling better?" he says.

"Yeah, I'm sorry about that, Tom, I just felt really anxious and panicky, I had to get some space."

Tom nods understandingly. "That's okay, I just didn't want you to miss anything. How you feeling about leaving?"

"Yeah, nervous. Really fucking nervous. I don't want to leave really," I say smiling.

Tom smiles back. "Trust me, everyone feels that way before leaving. I'm sure you'll be okay, bud, Just be vigilant and remember the advice we have given you. Just don't get cocky. Don't let yourself think even for a second that you are 'cured' Or you have 'cracked it'. Trust me, I have seen too many people come back through those doors because they thought they could drink again. Remember why you're here and why you want to be clean."

"I will. Thanks, Tom."

"No problem."

He gets up and pats me on the back.

He walks inside and out of view.

Twenty-four hours and I'm out of here.

Fuck.

Chapter 27: Home

I am in a car. I am laying in the back seat wrapped in a warm blanket. I can see my mum in the front seat driving. An orange glow flashes in through the window, the streetlights passing as we travel. I don't know where we are going, I don't know what time it is, but I feel safe. My mum is singing something to me.

"Close your eyes, and I'll miss you,
tomorrow I'll kiss you,
remember I'll always be true."

I recognise this song. It is making me feel calm. I feel sadness also, I don't know why.

"And while I am away,
I'll write home every day,
And I'll send all my loving to you…"

I wake up. I feel tears in my eyes. It's morning, my last morning here. That dream felt so real. When I was younger I would not be able to sleep. I would cry and scream out for my mum, because I was so scared of death and losing her. One night she picked me up out of bed, took me to the car and drove me around in the back seat, singing that song. I remember feeling so safe in that moment. It took away the thoughts in my head and for a while, just a small while, it was just me and her in that car. The terrifying thoughts I had, the loneliness of trying to sleep in my bed with those thoughts in my head were gone. I was just there, in that car, safe.

I get out of bed and check the time. I have slept in. It's eleven-thirty and it is a nice sunny day outside. I stand by the window and look out over the car park. I still can't believe in a short amount of time I will see my mum's car pull up and I will be going home. I feel that familiar lurch in my stomach. Nerves, a slight worry about going back out into the world. I try to brush it off. I put on some jogging bottoms and head downstairs.

"We-hey! Last day! How you feeling, mate?" Joe says.

He is standing in the living room, Abbie is sitting on the sofa and Pat is over at the dining table.

"Yeah, slightly shitting it!" I say.

Joe smiles. "You'll do great, mate, don't worry about it."

I smile in thanks. I walk over to the kitchen and make a cup of coffee.

"Going to miss you around here, Jack," Abbie says. She has followed me into the kitchen and is standing in the doorway.

"I'm going to miss all of you, I don't want to go if I'm honest! Really like it here," I say.

Abbie smiles and comes over to me.

"Just don't fuck it up!" she says into my ear. We both laugh and let go of one another. I notice she has tears in her eyes. This makes me feel sad but also touched. Abbie wipes her eyes and smiles, then walks out of the kitchen. I pick up my coffee and head out into the garden. I walk over to a bench in the sun, roll a cigarette and smoke.

It's so quiet here. I think I will miss that. Where I live isn't like it is here, there are streetlights and cars going by our house. Here there is nothing, just the sound of trees being blown by the wind and birds chirping. I see Mel through the window and she waves at me. I wave back. She comes outside and walks over to me.

"Leaving day!" she says, smiling.

"I know! Feels weird," I say.

"I've just come to get you as your mum's on the phone inside."

Mel beckons for me to follow her. I take a last drag on my cigarette, get up and follow her into the house. She points towards the phone booth outside the living room and I head over and pick it up.

"Mum?"

"Jacko! You okay, love?! You did it!"

"I know! I still can't believe it…"

My mum laughs happily down the phone. She sounds so happy. "Oh, love, we are all so proud of you. Listen, I will be there in about an hour so make sure you're packed. I can't tell you how proud of you I am, Jacko."

I feel tears coming.

"Thanks, Mum… wouldn't have been able to do it without you guys," I say, wiping my eyes.

"This was all you, love, so proud of you. I will see you soon, okay?"

"Sure, okay, love you, can't wait to see you," I say.

"Love you too, bye, love."

I put the phone down. I wipe my eyes again and head up the stairs to my room. I sit on my bed and look at the message I wrote to myself on the whiteboard. A message that gave me a lot of strength.

'YOU CAN DO THIS JACK' written shakily three times. I don't know why this helped me so much. I guess it's because I wrote it when I was genuinely at my lowest point. Terrified, lonely and lost. That first night feels a million years ago. Withdrawing and alone for the first time ever, and yet, I made it through. I smile at this thought and walk over to my bag in the corner of the room. I begin to pack up my clothes, leaving out a pair of jeans and a shirt to wear today. It doesn't take me long to pack everything I brought with me and I head out to have a shower.

Everyone is downstairs in group and I have the shower room to myself. I enter and stand under the hot water. I smile. I can't believe I'm leaving.

I get out, dry myself off and stand by the mirror. I examine my face. How much it has changed in such a short time. No more bags under my eyes, the colour has returned to my cheeks and I look reasonably healthy, for the first time in so, so long. I decide to have a shave and I take my time doing so.

I hear the other residents coming up the stairs outside. I wrap my towel around my waist and walk out of the bathroom.

"Here he is!" Craig says as he corners the stairs onto the landing.

I laugh. "Hey, man, how was group?" I say.

"Oh you know, same old shit." He smiles. "You excited to be leaving?"

"I am, mate, feels so weird to know that I'll be gone in less than an hour."

"Just stay in contact, keep yourself healthy, brother, you will be missed," he says. He pats me on the back and passes me.

I walk into my room, get dressed and double check I have everything packed. I hear a knock on the door.

"Your mum is downstairs, mate. How are you feeling?"

It's Tom. He walks into the room and sits on the edge of my bed. I feel a jolt of adrenaline surge through my gut.

"Yeah, I'm shitting myself," I say smiling. "I am excited though."

"You'll do well, buddy. Just stay strong and keep in contact with us so we know how you're getting on."

"I will, mate," I say.

He nods his head and looks around the room. "You know you didn't have to tidy up when you packed!" he says, laughing.

"To be honest it's been pretty neat most of my time here. It's quite a small space and I didn't want to get it mucky."

He laughs. "Well can you tell the others that before you leave!"

I laugh and he stands up.

"When you're ready, mate, come downstairs and say your goodbyes. Also we need to sign you out etcetera. That okay?"

"Sure. I'll come down now," I say.

I follow Tom out of the room and downstairs. A few of the residents are in the living room and I walk in to say goodbye.

"So that's me then," I say.

Abbie looks away from the TV and walks over to me. She hugs me tight.

"Good luck, mate, stay safe. I will write to you. What's your address?"

We aren't really supposed to give out personal information to other residents, but I do anyway. I pick up a pen and piece of paper off of a table near the door. I write my address and mobile number on it, then hand it back to Abbie.

"You take care of yourself, lovely," I say.

"Take care, brother," Craig says. He shakes my hand and winks. I smile.

Joe does he same and the other residents wave to me from their various seating places. I walk out of the living room and head towards the reception.

"Jack!"

I hear a voice calling my name from the games room and I double back. It's Mel. She is sitting down with Pat and they seem to be chatting. She excuses herself from Pat and walks over to me.

"Good luck! You nervous!?" she says, smiling.

"Bricking it," I say, laughing. "Very excited though, guess this is the real test now."

"I've got a good feeling about you my love, you'll do good things."

She hugs me and I hug her back.

"Thanks, Mel, thank you for all your help. Really appreciate it."

"Don't mention it," she says, grinning. I walk into the reception area and see my mum and brother standing there.

My mum smiles, tears in her eyes as I walk over and give her a long hug.

"Well done, sweetheart. I'm so proud of you! How are you feeling?" she says grinning ear to ear.

"Overwhelmed... I missed you guys so much!" I say. Tears are now flowing and I embrace my brother.

"So proud of you, Jacko, so proud."

"Thank you, brother, it's so good to see you, means the world," I say, smiling.

Tom comes into the reception area. He approaches my mum and shakes her hand.

"It's good to see you, Sue. Jack has done very well, now as I said to Jack, it's up to him. Hopefully he can continue the good work on the outside!"

My mum nods in agreement, still smiling.

"Thank you so much for all your help, Tom, I don't know where we would've been without your help. Really, thank you."

"It was our pleasure, Sue," he says smiling. "Now be good to your mum, she's a fucking saint and deserves an easy life now!" Tom says, smiling at me and packing me on the back.

"I couldn't agree more. Seriously thank you, Tom, thank you, all of you, for getting me better," I say, addressing the other key workers also in the room.

They all smile and say good luck. I lift up my bag and carry it out the front door. I walk down the steps, my mum linking my arm, and place my bag into the boot of the car. My brother pats me on the back, smiles and opens the front door of the car for me.

"Was going to say shotgun but thought that might be mean."

I laugh. I get in the front seat and start to roll a cigarette. It feels bizarre. The last time I was in this front seat was when I was on my way here. Drinking desperately and stressing about the impending situation. My mum climbs into the driver's seat and we start to pull out of the car park. I see the key workers at the door of the facility waving me goodbye. Abbie is by a window in the kitchen waving me off. I wave back and tears roll down my cheeks. I will miss this place a lot. I feel like I don't deserve the kindness I received there, but all the same, I am eternally grateful.

I feel sad I never got to say goodbye to Dev. He really helped me so much on that first night and I don't know how I would've coped without him. When I get home I will write a letter of thanks to him and to all the staff at Bridge House. Without them I would be dead, I am sure of it.

The journey back is strange. I put on some music and light up my cigarette. The movement of the car makes me feel slightly sick, like I haven't been in a moving vehicle for ages. I don't care though. I am so happy to be with my family.

"So good to have you back, Jacko, how do you feel?" my brother says from the back seat.

"Great, man, so good to be out, I feel a bit sad though as it was quite a safe place. I dunno, I feel weird," I say.

"That completely understandable, love..." my mum says, smiling at me. "At home your bed is all made up. I changed the room around because they say you need an environment that isn't the same one you drank in, I thought it would help!"

"That's so sweet, Mum, thank you so much," I say. She smiles back at me and holds my hand for a second between changing gears.

I can't believe I am fixed. I am not dying anymore. I can't believe it. I don't have to worry about when my next drink is, Whether or not I will withdraw or need to go to hospital. Let alone the other horrific stuff that came with drinking. It's over. It finally, is over.

Chapter 28: Adjusting

We turn into our road. It all feels surreal. The place is exactly the same but I am so different in my mind. I left home one person and I am returning a completely different one. We pull into our drive and immediately I am having flashbacks.

Running out of that same front door, brandishing a knife, swinging for invisible spectres that weren't there. I get out of the car and my mum opens the boot. I pick up my bag and stand in one spot. I roll a cigarette and smoke. I feel slightly dizzy. I feel nervous. I thought I would be happy to come home, I mean I am, but I feel so weird as well.

"Everything okay, love?" my mum says. She is smiling but looks slightly concerned.

"Yeah, I am okay, just feel nervous for some reason."

She nods her head and walks over to me. She links my arm again and walks with me towards the house.

"I know you have some bad memories here, but now is the time to make good ones. Your room looks all cosy and nice too. It'll be okay, love."

I nod my head in agreement and follow her inside.

It smells like home. I try to push out the bad memories for now. I want to enjoy this moment, I earned this moment. I follow my mum upstairs and she shows me my room. It looks beautiful. There is a small sofa at the end of my bed facing a TV on a coffee table. There are fairy lights all around the ceiling, and there are new bed sheets and a new duvet cover. Sitting on top of the duvet is a fresh set of pyjamas, laid out neatly. I smile. I turn and I hug my mum tightly.

"Thank you, Mum, I love you," I say.

" I love you too, Jacko."

I go and sit on my bed and take in the room. It really does look completely different. I am only noticing now, but there is a new colour paint on the walls as well. She really did all this in such a short time, it's so lovely. I get up and I roll another cigarette. I want to face my demons slightly. I want to go into the room I was in the most here, the front room downstairs. That room is where I hallucinated the most, also, where I spent most of my time drinking.

I walk down the stairs and I approach the door. I take a long breath in and out. I open the door.

It is tidy, but still smells faintly of cigarette smoke from all the times I smoked in here. The sofa sits to the right of me and the TV is opposite. I sit on the sofa. This is so bizarre. Just a few weeks ago, I was in this room, seeing dark hallucinations forming on the wall opposite me. This is where I heard the music coming from my fan and where I started really going into delirium tremens for the first time.

This room is where it all started and for now I hope, where it ends. Looking back on the hard times is very difficult. Lapping wine out of a plastic bag surrounded by broken glass, the hallucinations I witnessed, Super Alex, the woman who followed me up to my room in hospital, the seizures, the days without food, the sickness. Gone.

The gratitude I feel is something I can't describe. I owe my life to the doctors and nurses, key workers, mental health professionals and most of all, my family. I am one of the lucky ones. I had and I have a support network. This isn't something that everyone has. There are those out there who are dying, literally dying because of the stigma surrounding alcohol addiction. I owe my life to big hearted people, who don't see stigma, who just see a human in need of help. I really don't know what the future holds for me, if I think about it, it makes my head spin. I will remember Tom's words to me. Don't get cocky. I am not fixed, this story will never be over, take it day by day and expect the unexpected.

I will be vigilant and aware.

I will be forever grateful.